A S

American

Thought

Second Edition

Abraham Lincoln

Edited by John C. Powell

NEW FORUMS PRESS INC.

NEW FORUMS PRESS INC.

Published in the United States of America
by New Forums Press, Inc.
1018 S. Lewis St.
Stillwater, OK 74074
www.newforums.com

A Survey of American Thought, Second Edition

Library of Congress Cataloging-in-Publication Data Pending

This book may be ordered in bulk quantities at discount from New Forums
Press, Inc., P.O. Box 876, Stillwater, OK 74076 [Federal I.D. No. 73
1123239]. Printed in the United States of America.

International Standard Book Number: 1-58107-095-0

Cover design by Katherine Dollar.

Introduction

"The nation that wishes to remain free and ignorant, never was, and shall never be...." Thomas Jefferson

Thomas Jefferson is considered by many to be the man most responsible for promoting the idea of universal education in this country. Jefferson envisioned an educated population dominated by the Yeoman Farmer, who, through this education, would take his place among the governing bodies of state and federal governments. Jefferson's emphasis was on equal access to education: all male children of the citizens of the United States would have the opportunity for an education under Jefferson's plan. Jefferson emphasized opportunity because he realized that not all intellects are equal. It would be up to each individual to make the most of his intellectual gifts. He did not foresee that the outcome would be the same for each of us. While Jefferson's vision did not come to full fruition during his lifetime, the idea that all citizens have the right to an education is still a guiding principle in these United States.

Jefferson and the Founding Fathers wrote for posterity. They possessed a strong instinct that they were on the world stage, and that future generations would read their words and would judge each of them by these words. The result of this writing for history is that we are left with historical documents from the Founders which are meant to be read and debated not only in the context of the times in which they were written, but for our own time as well. The Founding Fathers felt they were creating a philosophy of government that should be debated for generations to come.

A Survey of American Thought aims to acquaint students of American history with the words of the men and women who have sought to shape American thought. Like the words of the

Founding Fathers, these words are meant to be read and debated. These words help us not only to understand their life and times, but to remind us of the principles by which we currently govern ourselves. Collectively, they constitute the basis for American democracy.

Students should evaluate each of the documents contained in this book and determine their meaning and value for our present generation. In many cases contrarian views are presented side by side in order to demonstrate how earlier generations debated certain issues. Students who read these documents may find a particular freshness and relevance to them. Just as Mr. Jefferson intended.

TABLE OF CONTENTS

INTRODUCTION ii

CHAPTER ONE 1
THE ROOTS OF AMERICAN DEMOCRACY 1
Mayflower Compact (1620) 3
FUNDAMENTAL ORDERS OF
CONNECTICUT (1639) 4
RHODE ISLAND CHARTER (1663) 4
MARYLAND TOLERATION ACT (1649) 5
PENNSYLVANIA CHARTER
OF PRIVILEGES (1701) 5
IDEAS OF THE ENLIGHTENMENT 6
Nicolaus Copernicus 6
Adam Smith 6
Isaac Newton 6
John Locke: Concerning Civil Government 6
The Natural Rights of Man 6
Benjamin Franklin: "Apology for Printers" 7
The Enlightenment: A Free Press 7

CHAPTER TWO 9
THE SPIRIT OF '76 9
Mercantilism 11
Question by British officials: 12
Answer by Governor Berkeley: 12
Question by British officials: 12
Answer by Governor Berkeley: 13
The Great Awakening: A "New Light" View 14
The Great Awakening: A Skeptical View 15
Two Views of Colonial Representative Government 17
A British View from Thomas Whately: 17
A Colonial View from the Providence Gazette: 17
Declaration and Resolves of the First
Continental Congress (1774) 19

American View of THE BATTLE
    OF LEXINGTON 1775 20
English View of THE BATTLE
    OF LEXINGTON 1775 21
Patrick Henry's Speech before the
    Virginia Convention (1775) 24
Thomas Paine's "The Crisis" (1776) 24
Thomas Paine's Common Sense 25
OF MONARCHY AND
    HEREDITARY SUCCESSION 25
THOUGHTS ON THE PRESENT
    STATE OF AMERICAN AFFAIRS 26
THE DECLARATION OF INDEPENDENCE 28

CHAPTER THREE 31
    THE CRITICAL PERIOD 31
Articles of Confederation (1781) 33
VIRGINIA STATUTE FOR
    RELIGIOUS FREEDOM (1786) 34
Northwest Ordinance (1787) 35
The Great Compromise of 1787 36
Constitution of the United States 38
THE FEDERALIST PAPERS 45
    NUMBER 1: HAMILTON 45
    NUMBER 39: MADISON 46
    NUMBER 10: MADISON 47
WASHINGTON'S FAREWELL
    ADDRESS OF 1796 51
Alexander Hamilton's Opinion of
    Thomas Jefferson May 26, 1792 54
Letter from Washington to Jefferson, 1797 54
Thomas Jefferson's Opinion of
    Alexander Hamilton May 23, 1792 55
Letter from Washington to Hamilton, 1792 55

CHAPTER FOUR 57
THE JEFFERSONIAN ERA 57
   Jefferson's First Inaugural Address (1801) 59
   The Republican View of the Federalists 60
   A Federalist View of Republicans 61
   Marbury v. Madison (1803) 62
   McCulloch v. Maryland (1819) 62
   Marshall on Interpreting the Constitution 63
   Monroe Doctrine (1823) 65

CHAPTER FIVE 67
THE JACKSONIAN ERA 67
   Jackson Attacks the Rich 69
   Frederick Jackson Turner on
    "Frontier Democracy" 70
   Jackson on Nullification 71
   Calhoun on the Nature of the Union 72
   The Removal of the Five Civilized Tribes 73
   Alexis De Tocqueville's *Democracy In America* 76

CHAPTER SIX 79
THE LITERARY AND REFORM MOVEMENTS 79
   Mankind 80
   Thoreau on Individualism 81
   Whitman on the American Genius 81
   De Tocqueville on American Reform 83
   The Seneca Falls Declaration 85

CHAPTER SEVEN 87
MANIFEST DESTINY AND
THE SLAVERY ISSUE 87
   Senator Corwin on Expansion 88
   President Polk on Expansion 88
   The Wilmot Proviso 89
   Popular Sovereignty 90
   A Pro-Slavery View 90

An Abolitionist View 91
Lincoln on the Slavery Question 92
Douglas on the Slavery Question 92
Uncle Tom's Cabin 94

CHAPTER EIGHT **95**
AN AMERICAN TRAGEDY:
CIVIL WAR AND RECONSTRUCTION **95**
South Carolina Secedes 96
Mr. Lincoln's First Inaugural Address 96
Lincoln to his Cabinet on Emancipation 98
Booker T. Washington
    on the Attainment of Freedom 98
Lincoln's Gettysburg Address (1863) 100
Lincoln's Second Inaugural Address 101
The Radical Plan of Reconstruction 102
Johnson's Veto of the Radical Plan 103

CHAPTER NINE **105**
THE SETTLEMENT OF THE WEST
AND INDUSTRIAL DEVELOPMENT **105**
Turner on the Frontier 106
The Sand Creek Massacre 107
Carnegie's *Gospel of Wealth* 110
President Grant to the Congress in 1876 111
How the Other Half Lives 113
Why Labor Unions are Necessary 116
The Farmer's Side (1891) 117
Populist Party Platform 118
Bryan's Cross of Gold Speech 122
Two Views on Blacks and Education 123
    Booker T. Washington 123
    W.E.B. DuBois 124
Nativist Views 124
    California Senator Miller, 1882 124
    Author Henry Pratt Fairchild,

Immigration, 1913 124
Author Madison Grant,
  The Passing of the Great Race, 1916 125
Author Edward A. Ross,
  Immigrants in Politics, early 1900s 125

CHAPTER TEN **127**
  IMPERIALISM **127**
    The Influence of Sea Power 128
    Two Positive Views on Imperialism 130
      Beveridge's Speech 130
      Adams's Speech 130
      The Anti-Imperialistic League (1899) 131
    Theodore Roosevelt's New Nationalism 133
      Theodore Roosevelt's
        "New Nationalism" Speech (1910) 133

CHAPTER ELEVEN **135**
  THE FIRST WORLD WAR **135**
    Wilson's New Freedom (1913) 136
    Wilson on American Ideals (1914) 137
    The Zimmermann Telegram 138
    Wilson's War Message (April 2, 1917) 139
    Senator Norris's Warning 140
    Wilson Supports the League 141
    Lodge Warns Against the League 142
    Palmer Speaks Against the Reds 143

CHAPTER TWELVE **145**
  PROSPERITY AND DEPRESSION **145**
    Mencken on the Ku Klux Klan 146
    Clarence Darrow Attacks Prohibition 147
    John Haynes Supports Prohibition 148
    The Kellogg Peace Pact (1928) 149
    Hoover on Rugged Individualism 151
    Hoover on Relief 153

Franklin D. Roosevelt on Relief.................. 154
Franklin D. Roosevelt's First
   Inaugural Address (1933).................. 155
The Socialist Party Platform of 1932 157
Huey Long's Share the Wealth Program (1933) 160
A Limiting View of Congressional Power 161
The National Labor Relations Act (1935) 163

CHAPTER THIRTEEN **165**
  WORLD WAR II **165**
    The Stimson Doctrine 166
    Gerald P. Nye: The Isolationist Viewpoint 167
    Franklin D. Roosevelt and
      The Contagion of War 167
    Franklin D. Roosevelt's
      "Four Freedoms" Speech (1941) 169
    An Anti-Lend-Lease View 170
    A Pro-Lend-Lease View 171
    Majority Report of Joint Committee
      on Pearl Harbor Attack 172
    The Internment of Japanese Americans 174
    A Plea Against Using the Bomb 175
    President Truman's View 176

CHAPTER FOURTEEN **177**
  THE COLD WAR **177**
    The Yalta Conference 179
    The Truman Doctrine 179
    Marshall Plan (1947) 180
    Proclamation of Philippine Independence (1946) 182
    McCarthy Attacks Marshall 183
    Dwight D. Eisenhower's
      Disarmament Proposals (1955).......... 184

CHAPTER FIFTEEN 187
THE STRUGGLE FOR CIVIL RIGHTS 187
    A Case for Segregation 188
    The Case against Segregation 189
    Brown v. Board of Education of Topeka, Kansas 190
    A Case for Violence 192
    A Case against Violence 193
    I Have a Dream 194
    A Statement from N.O.W. 195

CHAPTER SIXTEEN 197
POSTSCRIPTS 197
    John F. Kennedy's Inaugural Address (1961) 198
    The Gulf of Tonkin Resolution (1964) 199
    A Defense of Vietnam 200
    Speaking Out against Vietnam 201
    House Judiciary Committee (1974) 202

Chapter One
The Roots of American Democracy

"To understand political power, we must consider what state all men are naturally in, they are in a state of perfect freedom to order their actions, and dispose of their possessions and persons, as they think fit, within the bounds of the law of nature, without asking leave or depending upon the will of any other man."—John Locke

The voyage of the Mayflower to America was a dismal one. After several delays the Mayflower did not clear England until the autumn of 1620. The voyage lasted 64 days and almost ended in complete disaster as the ship approached the shores of Virginia. The winds and tides were so fierce that the ship was forced to head north to Cape Cod harbor. This steer northward was to have a profound impact not only on the Separatists (Puritans who wished to secede from the Church of England), but on the future of American democracy as well. These Separatists felt themselves no longer bound to the agreement they had signed when they left England; they were now in control of their own destiny. Before setting foot in the Cape Cod area these men drew up a document of self-government known as the *Mayflower Compact*. Like the male citizens of Jamestown, these Englishmen agreed to live under the rule of law and bound themselves into a body politic. The significance lies in the fact that by forming this political bond the Separatists had taken a major step towards breaking the European tradition of rule by the prince. The fact that the document was signed by virtually every male on board the Mayflower attests to the commitment of these men to self-government. The Separatists eventually settled in the area of Plymouth where it remained to put these ideas into practice. By the early eighteenth century, thirteen British colonies had been established. In each of the thirteen colonies a pattern of self-government was established. While giving homage to the British crown, the colonies found that the day to day necessity of protecting their citizens and meeting the demands of frontier life required citizen participation. A government housed three thousand miles away was impractical as a means of governing the diverse interests of the colonists.

Additionally, the eighteenth century saw the advent of an intellectual movement known as the Enlightenment. The Enlightenment, fueled by the writings of Isaac Newton and John Locke, stressed the concept of natural law. Newton had formulated a precise calculation of the workings of natural law on the universe, while Locke applied natural law to the human equation. To Locke, if natural law applied to planetary motion, it must necessarily apply to the actions of mankind. Natural law, according to Locke, includes the right to life, liberty, and property. The Enlightenment, coupled with the tendency towards self-government, would form a unique experiment that would culminate in the first modern democracy, The United States of America.

(The Mayflower Compact, signed by the Pilgrims in 1620, was not a plan of government in the traditional sense. It was a simple agreement among the Pilgrims to submit to the laws of the colony. However, it marks a major step in the development of self-government in the colonies.)

MAYFLOWER COMPACT (1620)

WE WHOSE NAMES are underwritten,...having undertaken...a voyage to plant the first colony in the northern parts of Virginia, do by these presents solemnly and mutually in the presence of God, and one of another, covenant and combine ourselves together into a civil body politic;...and by virtue hereof, to enact, constitute, and frame such just and equal laws, ordinances, acts, constitutions, and offices from time to time, as shall be thought most meet and convenient for the general good of the colony unto which we promise all due submission and obedience....

Define the following words which appear in the Mayflower Compact:

civil body politic
covenant
ordinance
acts
submission

(The first written constitution among the colonies was developed by Connecticut, in 1639. It consisted of eleven "fundamental orders.")

FUNDAMENTAL ORDERS OF CONNECTICUT (1639)

It is ordered…that there shall be yearly two general assemblies or courts:…first shall be called the Court of Election…

It is ordered…that no person be chosen governor above once in two years…

It is ordered…that to the aforesaid Court of Election the several towns shall send their deputies…

What is the purpose of a constitution?

(The first colonies did not practice religious toleration. The Puritans, who had come to the New World to escape religious persecution, were among the least tolerant. Gradually many of the colonies began to establish principles based on the concept of "freedom of worship.")

RHODE ISLAND CHARTER (1663)

No person within the said colony, at any time hereafter, shall be any wise molested, punished, disquieted, or called in question for any differences in opinion in matters of religion…but that all and every person and persons may, from time to time, and at all times hereafter, freely and fully have and enjoy his and their own judgments and consciences in matters of religious concernments…

MARYLAND TOLERATION ACT (1649)

Be it...enacted...that no person or persons...professing to believe in Jesus Christ shall...henceforth be any ways troubled, molested, or discountenanced...in respect of his or her religion nor in the free exercise thereof within this province...

PENNSYLVANIA CHARTER OF PRIVILEGES (1701)

I [Willliam Penn] do hereby grant and declare that no person or persons inhabiting...this province or territories who shall confess and acknowledge One Almighty God...shall be in any case molested or prejudiced in his or their person or estate because of his or their conscientious persuasion or practice...

What tie(s) can be seen between religious freedoms and the establishment of democracy in the colonies?

(The 1700s in Western Europe have been described as "the Age of the Enlightenment." This was a time when men were beginning to reevaluate their role in the universe. Ideas of equality, freedom, property rights, etc. were being intertwined with scientific advancements to literally form a new way of thinking. Nowhere was the Enlightenment more influential than in the American colonies.)

IDEAS OF THE ENLIGHTENMENT

Nicolaus Copernicus

"Finally we shall place the Sun himself at the center of the Universe...[in] the harmony of the whole Universe...."

Adam Smith

"It is the highest impertinence (for) kings and ministers to pretend to watch over the economy of the private people..."

Isaac Newton

"To every action there is always opposed an equal reaction..."

John Locke: Concerning Civil Government
The Natural Rights of Man

"To understand political power, we must consider what state all men are naturally in, they are in a state of perfect freedom to order their actions, and dispose of their possessions and persons, as they think fit, within the bounds of the law of nature, without asking leave or depending upon the will of any other man."

They are in a state also of equality, wherein all the power and jurisdiction is shared, no one have more than another.

But though this be a state of liberty, yet it is not a state of license; he has not liberty to destroy himself or any creature in his possession. The state of nature has a law of nature to govern it which obliges everyone, and reason, which is that law, teaches all mankind that no one ought to harm another in his life, health, liberty or possessions."

Benjamin Franklin: "Apology for Printers"
The Enlightenment: A Free Press

"Printers are educated in the belief that, when men differ in opinion, both sides ought equally to have the advantage of being heard by the public. When truth and error have fair play, the former is always an overmatch for the latter. Hence printers cheerfully serve all contending writers that pay them well, without regarding on which side they are of the question in dispute.

It is unreasonable to imagine that printers approve of everything they print. It is also unreasonable to censure them on any particular thing accordingly; since in the way of their business they print such great variety of things opposite and contradictory it is likewise unreasonable to hold that printers ought not to print anything but what they approve. If printers did that, an end would thereby be put to free writing."

Consider how the ideas of the Enlightenment helped to contribute to the development of democracy in the colonies.

Chapter Two
The Spirit of 76

"The Revolution was affected before the war commenced. The Revolution was in the minds and hearts of the people." John Adams, 1818

John Adams's statement that a Revolution had taken place in the minds and hearts of the American people long before the shots were fired at Lexington and Concord should not be construed to mean that the Revolution was inevitable. Even after the shots "heard around the world" were fired at Lexington and Concord, a majority of the Continental Congress and a good many American citizens, stood opposed to a declaration of independence. The now infamous *Olive Branch Petition* stands as evidence of the desire of America to reconcile with the mother country. By the summer of 1776 the notion of reconciliation would be put aside, as men like Thomas Paine, John Adams, and Thomas Jefferson embraced the notion of independence for the colonies.

The first truly revolutionary actions among the colonists stemmed from the inability of the British economic system of mercantilism to adequately serve the colonies. Prior to the French and Indian War (1754-1763), the colonists had been only nominally controlled by the British government. Indeed, when Adam Smith began writing his famous treatise *Wealth of Nations*, which advocated a laissez-faire economic system with no government interference, he pointed to the American colonies as an example of a free enterprise system at work. It is somewhat ironic that

Wealth of Nations was published in 1776, the year the colonists declared themselves the United States of America.

The French and Indian War had cost the British Crown dearly. After 1763 the British began to look at ways to pay for the continued protection of the American colonies. It seemed logical, from the British perspective, that these costs should at least be partially paid for by the colonists. Thus the policy of salutary neglect was ended. To the Americans, who were accustomed to virtually no government controls on their economic affairs, the new policies were an anathema. The conflict that we now call the American Revolution marks a turning point in world history. The American Revolution would not only bring about an independent American state, it would serve as a beacon to other peoples who sought relief from oppressive policies, most notably the French in 1789.

Mercantilism

And in regard his Majesties Plantations beyond the Seas are inhabited and peopled by his subjects of this His Kingdom of England, for the maintaining a greater correspondence and kindness between them and keeping them in a firmer dependance upon it, and rendering them yet more beneficial and advantageous unto it in the farther employment and Encrease of English Shipping and Seamen, vent of English Woollen and other Manufactures and Commodities rendering the Navigation to and from the same more safe and cheape, and making this kingdom a staple not only of the Commodities of those plantations but alsoe of the Commodities of ther countryes and Places for the supplying of them and it being the usage of other Nations to keepe their Trade to themselves. Be it enacted...that...noe Commoditie of the Growth Production or Manufacture of Europe shall be imported into any...Place to his Majestie belonging...but what shall be bona fide and without fraud laden and shipped in England Wales...and in English built Shipping...and which shall be carryed directly thence to the said Lands.

(From the Second Navigation Act, 1663)

Construct a definition of mercantilism

What restrictions were placed on the colonies?

Why would many merchants resent the Navigation Acts and other mercantilist policies?

(The comments below by Governor Berkeley of Virginia, in 1671, clearly show the resentment that was growing in the colonies over British mercantilist policy.)

Question by British officials:

"What obstructions do you find to the improvement of the trade and navigation of the plantations within your government?"

Answer by Governor Berkeley:

"Mighty and destructive, by that severe act of Parliament which excludes us having any commerce with any nation in Europe but our own, so that we cannot add to our plantation any commodity that grows out of it, as olive trees, cotton, or vines. Besides this, we cannot procure any skillful men for one now hopeful commodity, silk: for it is not lawful for us to carry a pipe stave, or a barrel of corn, to any place in Europe out of the king's dominions. If this were for His Majesty's service of the good of his subjects, we should not [complain] whatever our sufferings are for it; but on my soul, it is the contrary for both. And this is the cause why no small or great vessels are built here: for we are most obedient to all laws, whilst the New England men break through, and men trade to any place that their interest lead them."

Question by British officials:

"What advantages or improvement do you observe that may be gained to your trade or navigation?"

Answer by Governor Berkeley:

"None, unless we had liberty to transport our pipe staves, timber, and corn to other places besides the King's dominions."

Why does Governor Berkeley oppose British mercantilist policy?

(Religion played a dominant role in virtually all the colonies. Yet, as the Eighteenth century dawned, and people moved further into the frontier, organized religion began to lose some of its influence. The Great Awakening of the 1740' served to revive interest in religion in the Colonies. Some historians credit the Great Awakening with having helped to stir the fires of independence in the colonists.)

The Great Awakening: A "New Light" View

Now it pleased God to send Mr. Whitefield into this land...I longed to see and hear him, and wished he could come this way...then on a Sudden, in the morning about 8 or 9 of the Clock there came a messenger and said Mr. Whitefield preached at Hartford and Weathersfield yesterday and is to preach at Middletown this morning at ten of the Clock, I was in my field at Work, I...ran home to my wife telling her to make ready quickly to go and hear Mr. Whitefield preach at Middletown, then run to my pasture for my horse with all my might...when we came within about half a mile or a mile of the Road that comes down from Hartford Weathersfield and Stepney to Middletown; on high land I saw before me a Cloud or fogg rising; I first thought it came from the great River, but as I came nearer the Road, I heard a noise something like a low rumbling thunder and presently found it was the noise of Horses feet coming down the Road and this Cloud was a Cloud of dust made by the Horses feet; it arose some Rods into the air over the tops of Hills and trees and when I came within about 20 rods of the Road, I could see men and horses Slipping along in the Cloud like shadows and as I drew nearer it seemed like a steady Stream of horses and their riders, scarcely a horse more than his length behind another, all of a Lather and foam with sweat, their breath rolling out of their nostrils every Jump; every horse seemed to go with all his might to carry his rider to hear news from heaven for the saving of Souls, it made me tremble to see the sight, how the world was in a

Struggle and when we got to Middletown old meeting house there was a great Multitude it was said to be 3 or 4,000 of people Assembled together...When I saw Mr. Whitefield come upon the Scaffold he lookt almost Angelical; a young, Slim, slender youth before some thousands of people with a bold undaunted Countenance, and my hearing how God was with him every where as he came along it Solemnized my mind; and put me into a trembling fear before he began to preach; for he looked as if he was Cloathed with Authority from the Great God; and a sweet sollome solemnity sat upon his brow And my hearing him preach, gave me a heart wound; By Gods blessing; my old Foundation was broken up, and I saw that my righteousness would not save me. (From Nathan Cole, *"Spiritual Travels."* October 23, 1740.)

The Great Awakening: A Skeptical View

The Question is, whether it be'nt a plain, stubborn fact, that the Passions have, generally, in these Times, been apply'd to, as though the main Thing in Religion was to throw them into Disturbance? Can it be denied, that the Preachers, who have been the Instruments of the Commotions in the Land, have endeavoured, by all Manner of Arts, and in all Manner of Ways, to raise the Passions of their Hearers to such a Height, as really to unfit them, for the present, for the Exercise of their reasonable Powers? Nay, in order to alarm Men's Fears, has it not been common, among some Sort of Preachers, to speak and act after such a wild Manner, as is adapted to affrighten People out of their Wits, rather than possess their Minds of such a Conviction of Truth, as is proper to Men, who are endow'd with Reason and Understanding? And under the Notion of speaking to the Affections, were the Things of God and another World ever preached with more Confusion of Thought; with greater Incoherence; with the undue Mixture of more rash, crude, unguarded Expressions; or with Conceit to a higher Degree, appearing in fulsome Self-Applauses, as well as unheard of Contempt of others? These are Things of too publick a Nature to be denied: They have been too often practised, and in Places of too great Concourse, to admit of Debate.

(From Charles Chauncy, *Seasonable Thoughts on the State of Religion in New England,* 1743.)

What is the "New Light" view towards religion? The "Old Light" view?

Consider how the Great Awakening might have served to further the "independent mindedness" of the American colonists.

(As resentment over British economic policy grew, the phrase, "No taxation without representation," became very popular. The British claimed that the colonists were represented through Parliament (virtual representation). However, the colonists were seeking "actual representation" through their colonial assemblies.)

Two views of Colonial Representative Government
A British View from Thomas Whately:

"The fact is, that the inhabitants of the colonies are represented in Parliament; they do not indeed choose the members of that assembly; neither are nine-tenths of the people of Britain electors; for the right of election depends on property, voting customs, and to inhabitancy in some particular places.

The colonies are in exactly the same situation. All British subjects are really in the same; all are virtually represented in Parliament; for every member of Parliament sits in the House, not as Representative of his own constituents, but as one of that august assembly by which all the people of Great Britain are represented. As it is, the colonies and all British subjects whatever, have an equal share in the general representation in the House of Commons of Great Britain. Together, they are bound by the consent of the majority of that House, whether their own particular representatives consented to or opposed the measures voted upon or whether they had or had not particular Representatives there."

A Colonial View from the Providence Gazette:

"To infer that the British members (of Parliament) actually represent the colonies, who are not permitted to do the least act towards their appointment, although every man in the kingdom, who hath certain legal qualifications can vote for some one to represent him, is a piece of sophistry (trickery). Is there no dif-

17

ference between a country's having a privilege to choose 558 members to represent them in Parliament, and not having liberty to choose any? To turn the tables—if the Americans only had leave to send members to Parliament, could the people of Britain ever be persuaded that they were represented? ...national councils.

Suppose none of the 558 members were chosen by the people, but enjoyed the right of sitting in Parliament by hereditary descent, could the common people be said to share in the national councils? How insulting then is the argument, that we in America virtually have such share in the national councils, by those members whom we never chose? If we are not their constituents, they are not our representatives....It is really a piece of mockery to tell us that a country, detached from Britain, by an ocean of immense breadth, and which is so extensive and populous, should be represented by the British members, or that we can have any interest in the House of Commons."

Whose view was correct?

(On September 5, 1774, all the colonies (with the exception of Georgia), sent delegates to Philadelphia to discuss means of protest against the British. This delegation became known as the First Continental Congress. The main purpose for the meeting was to persuade the British to repeal the so-called "Intolerable Acts.")

Declaration and Resolves of the First Continental Congress (1774)

The Good People of the several colonies...declare...that the inhabitants of the English colonies in North America, by the immutable laws of nature, the principles of the English constitution, and the several charters or compacts, have the following rights:

Resolved,

That they are entitled to life, liberty, and property, and they have never ceded to any sovereign power whatever a right to dispose of either without their consent.

That our ancestors, who first settled these colonies, were at the time of their emigration from the mother country entitled to all the rights, liberties, and immunities of free and natural-born subjects within the realm of England...

That the foundation of English liberty and of all free government is a right in the people to participate in their legislative council...

What is the "tone" of this declaration by the First Continental Congress?

(On April 19, 1775, the "shots heard around the world" were fired at Lexington and Concord. Predictably, the accounts of what happened at Lexington and Concord vary. The historian faces the problem of choosing between two views.)

American View of THE BATTLE OF LEXINGTON...1775

Friends and fellow subjects—Hostilities are at length commenced in this colony by the troops under the command of General Gage, and it being of the greatest importance, that an early, true and authentic account of this inhuman proceeding should be known to you, the congress of this colony have transmitted the same, and from want of a session of the hon. continental congress, think it proper to address you on the alarming occasion.

By the clearest depositions relative to this transaction, it will appear that on the night preceding the nineteenth of April instant, a body of the king's troops, under the command of Colonel Smith, were secretly landed at Cambridge, with an apparent design to take or destroy the military and other stores, provided for the defence of this colony, and deposited at Concord—that some inhabitants of the colony, on the night aforesaid, whilst travelling peaceably on the road, between Boston and Concord, were seized and greatly abused by armed men, who appeared to be officers of General Gage's army; that the town of Lexington, by these means were alarmed, and a company of the inhabitants mustered on the occasion—that the regular troops on their way to Concord, marched into the said town of Lexington, and the said company, on their approach, began to disperse—that, notwithstanding this, the regulars rushed on with great violence and first began hostilities, by firing on said Lexington company, whereby they killed eight, and wounded several others—that the regulars continued their fire, until those of said company, who were neither killed nor wounded, had made their escape—that Colonel Smith, with the detachment then marched to Concord, where a number of provincials were again fired on by the troops, two of them killed and several wounded, before the provincials fired on them, and provincials were again fired on by the troops, produced an engagement that lasted through the day, in which many of the provincials and more of the regular troops were killed and wounded.

To give a particular account of the ravages of the troops, as they retreated from Concord to Charlestown, would be very difficult, if not impracticable; let it suffice to say, that a great number of the houses on the road were plundered and rendered unfit for use, several were burnt, women in child-bed were driven by the soldiery naked into the streets, old men peaceably in their houses were shot dead, and such scenes exhibited as would disgrace the annals of the most uncivilized nation.

These, brethren, are marks of ministerial vengeance against this colony, for refusing, with her sister colonies, a submission to slavery; but they have not yet detached us from our royal sovereign. We profess to be his loyal and dutiful subjects, and so hardly dealt with as we have been, are still ready, with our lives and fortunes, to defend his person, family, crown and dignity. Nevertheless, to the persecution and tyranny of his cruel ministry we will not tamely submit—appealing to Heaven for the justice of our cause, we determine to die or be free....

By order,
Joseph Warren, President

English View of the BATTLE OF LEXINGTON...1775

SIR,—In obedience to your Excellency's commands, I marched on the evening of the 18th inst. with the corps of grenadiers and light infantry for Concord, to execute your Excellency's orders with respect to destroying all ammunition, artillery, tents, &c, collected there, which were effected, having knocked off the trunnions of three pieces of iron ordnance, some new gun-carriages, a great number of carriage-wheels burnt, a considerable quantity of flour, some gun-powder and musquet-balls, with other small articles thrown into the river. Notwithstanding we marched with the utmost expedition and secrecy, we found this country had intelligence of strong suspicion of our coming, and fired many signal guns, and rung the alarm bells repeatedly; and were informed, when at Concord, that some cannon had been taken out of the town that day, that others, with some stores, had been carried three days before, which prevented our having an opportunity of destroying so much as might have been expected at our first setting off.

I think it proper to observe, that when I had got some miles on the march from Boston, I detached six light infantry companies to march with all expedition to seize the two bridges on different roads beyond Concord. On these companies' arrival at Lexington, I understand, from the report of Major Pitcairn, who was with them, and from many officers, that they found on a green closed to the road a body of the country people drawn up in military order, with arms and accoutrements, and, as appeared after, loaded; and that they had posted some men in a dwelling and Meeting-house. Our troops advanced towards them, without any intention of injuring them, further than to inquire the reason of their being thus assembled, and, if not satisfactory, to have secured their arms; but they in confusion went off, principally to the left, only one of them fired before he went off, and three or four more jumped over a wall and fired from behind it among the soldiers upon which the troops returned it, and killed several of them. They likewise fired on the soldiers from the Meeting and dwelling-houses....Rather earlier than this, on the road, a countryman from behind a wall had snapped his piece at Lieutenants Adair and Sutherland, but it flashed and did not go off. After this we saw some in the woods, but marched on to Concord without anything further happening. While at Concord we saw vast numbers assembling in many parts; at one of the bridges they marched down, with a very considerable body, on the light infantry posted there. On their coming pretty near, one of our men fired on them, which they returned; on which an action ensued, and some few were killed and wounded. In this affair, it appears that, after the bridge was quitted, they scalped and otherwise ill-treated one or two of the men who were either killed or severely wounded....On our leaving Concord to return to Boston, they began to fire on us from behind the walls, ditches, trees, &c., which, as we marched, increased to a very great degree, and continued without intermission for five minutes altogether, for, I believe, upwards of eighteen miles; so that I can't think but it must have been a preconcerted scheme in them, to attack the King's troops the first favorable opportunity that offered, otherwise, I think they could not, in so short a time from our marching out, have raised such a numerous body, and for so great a space of ground. Notwithstanding the enemy's numbers, they did not make one gallant attempt, during so long an action, though our men were so very fatigued, but kept under cover.

I have the honor, &c.,
F. Smith, Lieutenant-Colonel 10th Foot.

Compare the two accounts of the battle of Lexington. Which view has more credibility? Why do the views vary?

(Individuals played an important role in the revolution by inspiring others to back the conflict against England. Perhaps no words rang louder than those of Patrick Henry and Thomas Paine.)

Patrick Henry's Speech Before the Virginia Convention (1775)

Gentlemen may cry peace, peace. But there is no peace. The war is actually begun! The next gale that sweeps from the north will bring to our ears the clash of resounding arms! Our brethren are already in the field! Why stand we here idle? What is that gentlemen wish? What would they have? Is life so dear, or peace so sweet, as to be purchased at the price of chains and slavery? Forbid it, Almighty God! I know not what course others may take; but as for me, give me liberty or give me death!

Thomas Paine's "The Crisis" (1776)

These are the times that try men's souls. The summer soldier and the sunshine patriot will, in this crisis, shrink from the service of their country; but he that stands it now deserves the love and thanks of man and woman. Tyranny, like hell, is not easily conquered; yet we have this consolation with us, that the harder the conflict, the more glorious the triumph. What we obtain too cheap, we esteem too lightly; it is dearness only that gives everything its value. Heaven knows how to put a proper price upon its goods; and it would be strange indeed if so celestial an article as FREEDOM should not be highly rated....

What words of Patrick Henry's address have remained popular?

Who was Paine trying to appeal to in this excerpt from "The Crisis"?

(Published in January of 1776 (several months before the Declaration of Independence), Thomas Paine's Common Sense *inspired thousands of colonists to join the rebellion. Perhaps as many as 500,000 read* Common Sense.*)*

Thomas Paine's Common Sense
OF MONARCHY AND HEREDITARY SUCCESSION

Male and female are the distinctions of nature, good and bad the distinctions of Heaven, but how a race of men [that is, monarchs] came into the world so exalted above the rest, and distinguished like some new species, is worth inquiring into, and whether they are the means of happiness or of misery to mankind.

This is supposing the present race of kings in the world to have had an honorable origin. It is more than probable that, could we take off the dark covering of antiquity and trace them to their first rise, we should find the first of them nothing better than the principal ruffian of some restless gang, whose savage manners or preeminence in cunning obtained him the title of chief among plunderers, and who, by increasing in power and extending his depredations, over-awed the quiet and defenseless to purchase their safety by frequent contributions.

Monarchy and succession have laid, not this or that kingdom only, but the whole world in blood and ashes. 'Tis a form of government which the word of God bears testimony against, and blood will attend it.

The nearer any government approaches to a republic, the less business there is for a king. It is somewhat difficult to find a proper name for the government of England. Sir William Meridith calls it a republic, but in its present state it is unworthy of the name. The corrupt influence of the crown, having all positions at its disposal, has so effectually swallowed up the power and eaten out the virtue of the House of Commons (the republican part of the constitution) that the government of England is nearly as monarchial as that of France or Spain.

Men quarrel with names without understanding them. For 'tis the republican and not the monarchial parts of the constitution of England which Englishmen glory in—that is, the liberty of choosing a House of Commons from out of their own body. It is easy to see that when republican virtue fails, slavery ensues. Why is the constitution of England sickly? Because monarchy has poisoned the republic; the crown has absorbed the commons.

THOUGHTS ON THE PRESENT STATE OF AMERICAN AFFAIRS.

I challenge the warmest advocate for reconciliation to show a single advantage that this continent can reap by being connected with Great Britain. I repeat the challenge: not a single advantage is derived. Our grain will fetch its price in any market in Europe and our imported goods must be paid for, buy them where we will. But the injuries and disadvantages we sustain by that connection are without number, and our duty to mankind at large, as well as to ourselves, instruct us to renounce the alliance.

Everything that is right or reasonable pleads for separation. The blood of the slain, the weeping voice of nature cries, TIS TIME TO PART. Even the distance at which the Almighty has placed England and America is a strong and natural proof that the authority of the one over the other was never the design of Heaven. The time likewise at which the continent was discovered adds weight to the argument, and the manner in which it was peopled increases the force of it. The Reformation was preceded by the discovery of America, as if the Almighty graciously meant to open a sanctuary to the persecuted in future years, when home should afford neither friendship nor safety.

But where, say some is the king of America? I'll tell you, friend: he reigns above, and does not make havoc of mankind like the Royal Brute of Great Britain. Yet, that we may not appear to be defective even in earthly honors, let a day be solemnly set apart for proclaiming the Charter. Let it be brought forth, placed on the Divine Law, the Word of God. Let a crown be placed thereon, by which the world may know that so far as we approve of monarchy, in America THE LAW IS KING. For as in absolute governments the king is law, so in free countries the law ought to be king and there ought to be no other.

(From Thomas Paine, *Common Sense*: Addressed to the Inhabitants of America. Philadelphia: J. Almon, 1776)

On what grounds does Paine attack the English monarchy?

What reasoning does Paine use in calling for a break with England?

(It was Richard Henry Lee of Virginia who proposed in June of 1776 that "resolutions" should be drawn up stating that the colonies ought to be "free and independent states." Consequently, a committee consisting of John Adams, Benjamin Franklin, and Thomas Jefferson was authorized by the Continental Congress to issue a "Declaration of Independence." Jefferson did most of the actual writing of the document (with Adams and Franklin serving as editors).

THE DECLARATION OF INDEPENDENCE

In Congress, July 4, 1776

THE UNANIMOUS DECLARATION OF THE THIRTEEN UNITED STATES OF AMERICA.

When in the Course of human events, it becomes necessary for one people to dissolve the political bands which have connected them with another, and to assume among the Powers of the earth, the separate and equal station to which the Laws of Nature and of Nature's God entitle them, a decent respect to the opinions of mankind requires that they should declare the causes which impel them to the separation.

We hold these truths to be self-evident, that all men are created equal, that they are endowed by their Creator with certain unalienable Rights, that among these are Life, Liberty and the pursuit of Happiness. That to secure these rights, Governments are instituted among men, deriving their just powers from the consent of the governed, That whenever any Form of Government becomes destructive of these ends, it is the Right of the People to alter or to abolish it, and to institute new Government, laying its foundation on such principles and organizing its powers in such form, as to them shall seem most likely to effect their Safety and Happiness. Prudence, indeed, will dictate that Governments long established should not be changed for light and transient causes; and accordingly all experience hath shown, that mankind are more disposed to suffer, while evils are sufferable, than to right themselves by abolishing the forms to which they are accustomed. But when a long train of abuses and usurpations, pursuing invariably the same Object evinces a design to reduce them under absolute Despotism, it is their right, it is their duty, to throw off such Government, and to provide new Guards for their future security.—Such has been the patient sufferance of these Colonies; and such is not the necessity which constrains them to alter their former Systems of Government. The history of the present King of great Britain is a history of repeated injuries and usurpations, all having in direct object the establishment of an absolute tyranny over these States. To prove this, let Facts be submitted to a candid world.......

Examine other documents and determine if the "Declaration of Independence" is a wholly original document.

Chapter Three
The Critical Period

"Each state retains its sovereignty, freedom, and independence, and every power, jurisdiction, and right which is not by this confederation expressly delegated to the United States in Congress assembled." —Articles of Confederation, 1781

When the *Declaration of Independence* was ratified by the Continental Congress on July 4, 1776, the United States of America was born. Historians were quick to point out that the unity was in name only. George Washington complained bitterly during the Revolution about the lack of funding for his army. It is in large part due to the leadership of Washington that a Continental Army was maintained throughout the War for Independence. Most colonists, including the majority of the delegates to the Continental Congress, were committed primarily to their individual states. The "every state for itself" attitude did not bode well for colonial victory. To help provide for a more stable United States a new constitution to govern the states was proposed by a congressional delegation. Ratified in 1781, this constitution became known as the *Articles of Confederation*.

While the *Articles of Confederation* had some successes, most notably ending the Revolutionary War via the Peace of Paris in 1783, and settling the potentially disastrous Western land conflicts among the various states, it proved itself incapable of handling the myriad of problems that sprang up between the states after the Revolution ended. Trade disputes, treaty negotiations, and alarming uprisings within the states proved too much for the new government to handle. The problem resided in the wording of the *Articles of Confederation*. The emphasis was on the autonomy of each state. The states were reluctant to pay taxes to a national government that few of its citizens believed in. There was no president, and no national army. By the time the Constitutional Convention convened in 1787, the Continental Congress had ceased to be a viable entity.

When farmers in Western Massachusetts, led by a certain Daniel Shays, used mob violence to protest tax policy, the weaknesses of *The Articles* became even more evident. As Shays and his fellow farmers blocked the sitting of four courts in Western Massachusetts and threatened to march on the Massachusetts statehouse, there was no federal army to turn to for help. Alarmed by the impotence of the federal government, factions led by men like Alexander Hamilton, began to agitate for a revision of *The Articles* to correct certain inherent weaknesses. When fifty-five delegates from eleven states (Rhode Island refused to participate) met in Philadelphia in 1787 to revise *The Articles*, there was little indication of what was about to take place. Instead of a mere revision of *The Articles of Confederation*, a wholly new document was created—*The Constitution of the United States of America*. This constitution has lasted for over two hundred years.

(The Articles of Confederation *were designed to place the power of government with the states, and not with a federal government. Even a cursory examination of the Articles reveals certain "inherent weaknesses" that made them unsuitable for a young nation striving to take its place among the ruling nations of the world.)*

Articles of Confederation (1781)

Article 1. The style of this confederacy shall be "The United States of America."

Article 2. Each state retains its sovereignty, freedom, and independence, and every power, jurisdiction, and right which is not by this confederation expressly delegated to the United States in Congress assembled.

Article 3. The said states hereby severally enter into a firm league of friendship with each other for their common defense, the security of their liberties, and their mutual and general welfare, binding themselves to assist each other against all force offered to or attacks made upon them or any of them on account of religion, sovereignty, trade, or any other pretense whatever....

What powers were retained by the various states under the Articles of Confederation?

According to Article 3, what was the main purpose for states to enter into this agreement?

Examine the Articles of Confederation *in their complete form. Point out some of the weaknesses of the Articles.*

(The states provided many documents from which the framers of the Constitution could draw. One of the most important was the Virginia Statute for Religious Freedom, which was written in 1786. Interestingly, the State of Virginia, led by Thomas Jefferson, would later push for a Bill of Rights to be added to the Constitution.)

VIRGINIA STATUTE FOR RELIGIOUS FREEDOM (1786)

Well aware that Almighty God has created the mind free; that all attempts to influence it by temporal punishments...tend only to...habits of hypocrisy and meanness...to compel a man to furnish contributions of money for the propagation of opinions which he disbelieves is sinful and tyrannical;...truth is great and will prevail if left to herself....

...no man shall be compelled to frequent or support any religious worship...whatsoever;...all men shall be free to profess...their opinion in matters of religion;...the same shall in no way diminish, enlarge, or affect their civil capacities....

Why is the Virginia Statute for Religious Freedom *important?*

(One of the most important accomplishments of the American government under the Articles of Confederation was the passage of the Northwest Ordinance. *Not only did the Northwest Ordinance provide for the governance of the northwest territory, it established certain democratic principles which would be of great importance in the development of the American frontier.)*

NORTHWEST ORDINANCE (1787)

Article 1. No person...shall ever be molested on account of his mode of worship or religious sentiments....

Article 2. The inhabitants of the said territory shall always be entitled to the benefits of the writ of habeas corpus and of the trial by jury....

Article 3. Religion, morality, and knowledge being necessary to good government and the happiness of mankind, schools and the means of education shall forever be encouraged. The utmost good faith shall always be observed toward the Indians....

Article 6. There shall be neither slavery nor involuntary servitude in the said territory, otherwise than in punishment of crimes....

What are the "democratic" principles set forth by the Northwest Ordinance?

Why would this document be important to future generations of Americans?

(The constitutional convention met from May to September of 1787. Ostensibly, its purpose was to "revise" the Articles of Confederation. The fifty-five delegates sent by the states (except Rhode Island) to the convention soon found themselves in position to rewrite the entire document. The result was a document radically different from the Articles. Many compromises had to be reached before this new document was completed. Some of the most bitter debates centered on the question of congressional representation. The so-called Connecticut Compromise settled this question, reaching a settlement that was acceptable to both large and small states.)

THE GREAT COMPROMISE OF 1787

THURSDAY JUNE 21 IN CONVENTION

Doctr. Johnson. On a comparison of the two plans which had been proposed from Virginia and New Jersey, it appeared that the peculiarity which characterized the latter was its being calculated to preserve the individuality of the states. The plan from Virginia did not profess to destroy this individuality altogether, but was charged with such a tendency. One gentleman alone (Colonel Hamilton) in his criticisms of the plan of New Jersey, boldly and decisively contended for an abolition of the state governments. Mr. Wilson and the gentleman from Virginia who also were adversaries of the plan of New Jersey held a different language. They wished to leave the states in possession of a considerable, tho' a subordinate, jurisdiction. They had not yet, however, shown how this could be consistent with, or be secured against, the general sovereignty and jurisdiction which they proposed to give to the national government. If this could be shown in such a manner as to satisfy the patrons of the New Jersey propositions (that the individuality of the states would not be endangered), many of their objections would no doubt be removed. If this could not be shown, their objections would have their full force.

FRIDAY JUNE 29 IN CONVENTION
Doctr. Johnson. The controversy must be endless whilst gentlemen differ in the grounds of their arguments. Those on one side consider the states as districts of people composing one political society; those on the other consider them as so many political societies. The fact is that the states do exist as political societies, and a government is to be formed for them in their political capacity, as well as for the individuals composing them. Does it not seem to follow, that if the states as such are to exist they must be armed with some power of self-defense? This is the idea of (Colonel Mason) who appears to have looked to the bottom of this matter. Besides the aristocratic and other interests, which ought to have the means of defending themselves, the states have their interests as such, and are equally entitled to like means. On the whole he thought that as in some respects the states are to be considered in their political capacity, and in others as districts of individual citizens, the two ideas embraced on different sides, instead of being opposed to each other, ought to be combined. In one branch the people ought to be represented; in the other, the states.

Adapted from The Records of the Federal Convention of 1787

Explain the compromise(s) reached by this agreement.

(Abraham Lincoln once stated. "We should read the Constitution every day. It is God's gift to these United States." It is the oldest written constitution in continual use in the world today.)

CONSTITUTION OF THE UNITED STATES
(Framed in 1787; adopted, 1788)

Preamble: (define and discuss)

Article I. The Legislative Branch

Section 1. Congress

1. legislative power
2. bicameral

Section 2. House of Representatives

1. Election and term of members
2. Qualifications
3. Apportionment of Representatives and Direct Taxes
   a. apportion
   b. 3/5's compromise
   c. each state gets one Representative
   d. today's apportionment
   e. the role of the census
4. Filling vacancies ("writs of election")
5. Officers; impeachment
   a. Speaker and other officers
   b. impeach

Section 3. Senate

1. Number of members and term of office

2. Classification; filling vacancies (a continuing body)
   a. "staggered terms"
   b. filling vacancies
3. Qualifications
4. President of the Senate
5. Other Senate offices (Pro Tempore)
6. Trial of impeachments
   a. Senate tries
   b. role of the Chief Justice in Presidential impeachment trials
   c. 2/3's needed to convict on impeachment charges
7. Penalty for conviction
   a. indictment
   b. does not extend to criminal conviction (refers to impeachment trial)

Section 4. Election and Meetings

1. Holding elections (when?)
2. meetings (once per year; now changed to January 3rd)

Section 5. Rules of Procedure

1. Organization (define quorum)
2. Proceedings (each house determines its own rules)
3. Journals must be kept ("Congressional Record")
4. Adjournment (must have each other's permission)

Section 6. Privileges and Restrictions

1. Pay and privileges
2. How a bill becomes a law
   a. House to Senate to President
   b. veto; 2/3's vote needed to override a veto
   c. pocket veto
   d. President has ten days to sign a bill or it becomes law

3. Presidential approval or veto
   a. orders and resolutions
   b. joint resolutions
   c. concurrent resolutions

Section 8. Powers Delegated To Congress

1. tax power
2. power to borrow
3. commerce power
4. naturalization and bankruptcy
5. coin money, standards of weights and measures
6. power to punish counterfeiters
7. establish post offices and post roads
8. patents and copyrights
9. establish "inferior" courts
10. to control its citizens even when they are out of the country
11. to declare war (grant letters of marque)
12. to support armies
13. to provide a navy
14. to establish rules for the military
15. to call out the militia
16. to help states support the militia
17. to control the D.C. area (note: D.C. was not established yet)
18. "necessary and proper clause"

Section 9. Powers Denied to the Federal Government

1. refers to slave importation (please note the years involved here)
2. habeas corpus
3. bill of attainder and ex-post facto laws
4. capitation tax (altered by the 16th amendment)
5. exports from states
6. equal trade guaranteed

7. "power of the purse"
8. titles of nobility

Section 10. Powers Denied to the States

Since most of these are the same as those denied to the federal government, we will simply summarize here.

ASSIGNMENT: Go back and read Article I of the Constitution. After reading, come up with ten questions, words, etc. that you have over Article I.

Article II. The Executive Branch

Section 1. President and Vice-President

1. Term of office
2. Electoral College
   a. equal to congressional representation
   b. electors cannot hold office or get profit
3. Method of using electoral system
   a. each elector gets two votes (note 12th amendment)
   b. President of Senate holds count
   c. non-electoral majority House chooses President Senate VP (vote by states not individuals)
4. Time of elections
5. Qualifications (35, natural born, 14 years a resident)
6. Filling vacancies ("order of succession")
7. Salary
8. Oath of office (read)

Section 2. Powers of the President

1. Military powers (Commander in Chief)
   a. executive offices (may dismiss without consent of Congress)

41

2. Treaties and Appointments
   a. advise and consent (2/3 vote of Senate needed for treaties)
   b. all appointments need Senate approval (judges, ambassadors, etc.)
3. Filling vacancies (until Senate returns)

Section 3. Duties of the President

1. State of the union; may adjourn Congress; receives Ambassadors, executes the law.

Section 4. Impeachment

Article III . Judicial Branch

Section 1. Federal Courts

1. establishes the Supreme Court ("inferior" courts)

Section 2. Jurisdiction of the Courts

1. General jurisdiction (law and equity, two or more states, etc. read)
2. Supreme Court (original vs. appellate)
3. Conduct of trials (read)

Section 3. Treason

1. definition of treason (read)
2. punishment (corruption of blood; forfeiture)

Article IV. Relationships among the States

Section 1. Official Acts

1. States must recognize each others' official records.

Section 2. Privileges of Citizens

1. Each state must respect the rights of citizens from another state.
2. Extradition
3. Fugitive slaves (of historical significance only)

Section 3. New States and Territories

1. How states are admitted
2. Congress has power over territories and government property

Section 4. Guarantees to the States

1. A "republican" form of government guaranteed to every state. (Concept of martial law)

Article V.

Methods of Amending the Constitution	Methods of Ratification
1. 2/3's vote of Congress	1. 3 /4's of State Legislatures
2. 2/3's vote by State Legislatures	2. 3 /4's vote by States by convention

Article VI. General Provisions

1. All debts honored by the national government
2. The Supreme law of the land!!!
3. Oaths of office
   (All federal officers and state legislators must uphold the constitution; but no religious test shall be required.)

Article VII. Ratification

1. Nine of thirteen states needed to ratify the constitution
   The ninth state ratified the Constitution in 1788. All thirteen eventually voted for ratification.

(The Federalist Papers were written by Alexander Hamilton, John Jay, and James Madison in an effort to persuade the State of New York to accept the newly written constitution. The Federalist Papers give us an excellent description of American federalism.)

THE FEDERALIST PAPERS

Number 1: Hamilton

After an unequivocal experience of the inefficacy of the subsisting federal government, you are called upon to deliberate on a new Constitution for the United States of America. The subject speaks its own importance; comprehending in its consequences nothing less than the existence of the UNION, the safety and welfare of the parts of which it is composed, the fate of an empire in many respects the most interesting in the world. It has been frequently remarked that it seems to have been reserved to the people of this country, by their conduct and example, to decide the important question, whether societies of men are really capable or not of establishing good government from reflection and choice, or whether they are forever destined to depend for their political constitutions on accident and force. If there be any truth in the remark, the crisis at which we are arrived may with propriety be regarded as the era in which that decision is to be made; and a wrong election of the part we shall act may, in this view, deserve to be considered as the general misfortune of mankind....

I propose, in a series of papers, to discuss the following interesting particulars:—The utility of the UNION to you, political prosperity—The insufficiency of the present Confederation to preserve the Union—The necessity of a government at least equally energetic with the one proposed to the attainment of this object—The conformity of the proposed Constitution to the true principles of republican government—its analogy to your own State constitution—and lastly, The additional security which its adoption will afford to the preservation of that species of government, to liberty, and to property. In the progress of this discussion I shall endeavor to give a satisfactory answer to all the objections which shall have made their appearance, that may seem to have any claim to your attention.

It may perhaps be thought superfluous to other arguments to prove the utility of the UNION...But the fact is that we already hear it in the private circles of those who oppose the new Constitution, that the thirteen States are of too great extent for any general system, and that we must of necessity resort to separate confederacies of distinct portions of the whole...[but] nothing can be more evident to those who are able to take an enlarged view of the subject than the alternative of an adoption of the new Constitution or a dismemberment of the Union...Publius.

Number 39: Madison

...we may define a republic to be...a government which derives all its powers directly or indirectly from the great body of the people and is administered by persons holding their offices during pleasure for a limited period, or during good behavior. It is essential to such a government that it be derived from the great body of the society, not from an inconsiderable proportion or a favored class of it; otherwise a handful of tyrannical nobles, exercising their oppression by a delegation of their powers, might aspire to the rank of republicans and claim for their government the honorable title of republic. It is sufficient for such a government that the persons administering it be appointed either directly or indirectly, by the people; and that they hold their appointments by either of the tenures just specified...

On comparing the Constitution planned by the convention with the standard here fixed, we perceived once that it is, in the most rigid sense, conformable to it...

...In order to ascertain the real character of the government, it may be considered in relation to the foundation on which it is to be established; to the source from which its ordinary powers are to be drawn; to the extent of them; and to the authority by which future changes in the government are to be introduced.

On examining the first relation, it appears, on one hand, that the Constitution is to be founded on the assent and ratification of the people of America, given by deputies elected for the special purpose; but, on the other that this assent and ratification is to be given by the people, not as individuals composing one entire nation, but as composing the distinct and independent States to which they respectively belong. It is to be the assent and ratification of the several States, derived from the supreme authority in each State—the authority of the people themselves. The act, therefore, establishing the Constitution will not be a national but a federal act...

The next relation is to the source from which the...powers of government are to be derived. The House of Representatives will derive its powers from the people of America; and the people will be represented in the same proportion and on the same principle as they are in the legislature of a particular State. So far the government is national, not federal. The Senate, on the other hand, will derive its powers from the States as political and coequal societies; and these will be represented on the principle of equality in the Senate, as they now are in the existing Congress [under the Articles of Confederation]. So far the government is federal, not national....

Number 10: Madison

Among the numerous advantages promised by a well-constructed Union, none deserves to be more accurately developed than its tendency to break and control the violence of faction....

By a faction I understand a number of citizens, whether amounting to a majority or minority of the whole, who are united and actuated by some common impulse of passion, or of interest, adverse to the rights of other citizens, or to the permanent and aggregate interests of the community....

If a faction consists of less than a majority, relief is supplied by the republican principle, which enables the majority to defeat its sinister views by regular vote. It may clog the administration, it may convulse the society; but it will be unable to execute and mask its violence under the forms of the Constitution. When a majority is included in a faction, the form of popular government...enables it to sacrifice to its ruling passion or interest both the public good and the rights of other citizens. To secure the public good and private rights against the danger of such a faction, and at the same time to preserve the spirit and the form of popular government, is then the great object to which our inquiries are directed...

By what means is this object attainable? Evidently by one of two only. Either the existence of the same passion or interest in a majority at the same time must be presented, or the majority having such coexistent passion or interest, must be rendered, by their number and local situation, unable to concert and carry into effect schemes of oppression....

From this view of the subject it may be concluded that a pure democracy, by which I mean a society consisting of a small number of citizens, who assemble and administer the government in person, can admit of no cure for the mischiefs of faction. A common passion or interest will, in almost every case, be felt by a majority of the whole...and there is nothing to check the inducements to sacrifice the weaker party or an obnoxious individual. Hence it is that such democracies have ever been spectacles of turbulence and contention; have ever been found incompatible with personal security or the rights of property; and have in general been as short in their lives as they have been violent in their deaths. Theoretic politicians, who have patronized the species of government, have erroneously supposed that by reducing mankind to a perfect equality in their political rights, they would at the same time be perfectly equalized and assimilated in their possessions, their opinions, and their passions.

A republic, by which I mean a government in which the scheme of representation takes place, opens a different prospect and promises the cure for which we are seeking. Let us examine the points in which it varies from pure democracy, and we shall comprehend both the nature of the cure and the efficacy which it must derive from the Union.

The two great points of difference between a democracy and a republic are: first, the delegation of the government, in the latter, to a small number of citizens elected by the rest; secondly, the greater number of citizens and greater sphere of country over which the latter may be extended. The effect of the first difference is, on the one hand, to refine and enlarge the public views by passing them through the medium of a chosen body of citizens, whose wisdom may best discern the true interest of their country and whose patriotism and love or justice will be least likely to sacrifice it to temporary or partial considerations. Under such a regulation it may well happen that the public voice, pronounced by the representatives of the people, will be more consonant to the public good than if pronounced by the people themselves, convened for the purpose. On the other hand, the effect may be inverted. Men of factious tempers, of local prejudices, or of sinister designs may by intrigue, by corruption, or by other means, first obtain the suffrages and then betray the interests of the people. The question resulting is, whether small or extensive republics are most favorable to the election of proper guardians of the public wealth....

Study Questions for the Federalist Papers

#1.   MAIN IDEAS IN THE FEDERALIST PAPERS

1. What was the "crisis at which we have arrived" that is mentioned in the first paragraph of this essay?

2. Why, according to "publius," would a "...wrong election of [decision about] the part we shall act...[in response to the "crisis"] deserve to be considered as the misfortune of mankind?

3. In your own words, what were the main goals of the Federalist Papers?

#39.   FEDERALISM AND REPUBLICANISM IN THE FEDERALIST PAPERS

1. What is Madison's definition of a republic?

2. Explain Madison's definition of federalism, which is based on the idea that the   Constitution of 1787 is a "composition of both" federal and national characteristics?

#10.   FEDERALISM AND POPULAR SOVEREIGNTY

1. What are the main differences between a republic and a democracy?

2. What are the dangers of a pure or unlimited democracy?

3. How does a republic overcome weaknesses associated with pure democracy?

(George Washington has been described as the "indispensable man." His farewell address in 1796 is considered one of the most important presidential messages in American history. It is a document still referred to today.)

WASHINGTON'S FAREWELL ADDRESS OF 1796

"Every part of our country feels an immediate and particular interest in union, all the parts combined cannot fail to find in the united mass of means and efforts greater strength, greater resource, proportionably greater security from external danger, a less frequent interruption of their peace by foreign nations and, what is of inestimable value, they must derive from union an exemption from wars between themselves.

I have already intimated to you the danger of parties in the State, with particular reference to the founding of them on geographical discrimination.

The alternative domination of one faction over another, sharpened by the spirit of revenge, natural to party dissension, is itself a frightful despotism. But this leads at length to a more formal and permanent despotism. The disorders and miseries which result, gradually incline the minds of men to seek security and repose in the absolute power of an individual; and sooner or later the chief of some prevailing faction, more able or more fortunate than his competitors, turns this disposition to the purposes of his own elevation, on the ruins of public liberty.

Parties serve always to distract the public councils, and enfeeble the public administration. It agitates the community with ill-founded jealousies and false alarms; kindles the animosity of one part against another, foments occasionally riot and insurrection. It opens the doors to foreign influence and corruption, which find a facilitated access to the government itself through the channels of party passions.

As a very important source of strength and security, cherish public credit. One method of preserving it is, to use it as sparingly as possible; avoiding occasions of expense by cultivating peace, but remembering also that timely disbursements to prepare for danger frequently prevent much greater disbursements to repel it; which we ourselves ought to bear. The execution of these maxims belong to your representatives, but it is necessary that public opinion should cooperate. To have revenue there must be taxes; that no taxes can be devised which are not more or less inconvenient and unpleasant.

Observe good faith and justice towards all nations; cultivate peace and harmony with all. Religion and morality enjoin this conduct.

The nation which indulges towards another an habitual hatred, or an habitual fondness, is in some degree a slave. It is a slave to its animosity or to its affection, either of which is sufficient to lead it astray from its duty and its interest.

As avenues to foreign influence in innumerable ways, such attachments are particularly alarming to the truly enlightened and independent patriot.

Against the insidious wiles of foreign influence, the jealousy of a free people ought to be constantly awake, since history and experience prove that foreign influence is one of the most baneful foes of republican government.

Excessive partiality for one foreign nation, and excessive dislike of another, cause those whom they actuate to see danger only on one side, and serve to veil and even second the arts of influence on the other.

The great rule of conduct for us in regard to foreign nations is, in extending our commercial relations, to have with them as little political connection as possible. So far as we have already formed engagements, let them be fulfilled with perfect good faith. Here let us stop.

Our detached and distant situation invites and enables us to pursue a different course.

Why, by interweaving our destiny with that of any part of Europe, entangle our peace and prosperity in the toils of European ambition, rivalship, interest, humor or caprice?

It is our true policy to steer clear of permanent alliances with any portion of the foreign world."

(Adapted from Washington's 1796 address)

What did Washington have to say on the following subjects:

a. *taxes;*

b. *political parties;*

c. *foreign policy?*

(Thomas Jefferson and Alexander Hamilton, both members of Washington's first cabinet were at opposite ends of the political spectrum. From their disputes sprang the first political parties.)

ALEXANDER HAMILTON'S OPINION OF THOMAS JEFFERSON MAY 26, 1792:

"I became...convinced of the following truth, that Mr. Madison, co-operating with Mr. Jefferson, is at the head of a faction, decidedly hostile to me, and my administration; and [motivated] by views, in my judgment, subversive of the principles of good government, and dangerous to the Union, peace and happiness of the country...In various conversations with foreigners, as well as citizens, he [Jefferson] has thrown censure on my principles of government, and on my measures of administration....Another circumstance has contributed to widening the breach. "Tis evident beyond a question, from every moment, that Mr. Jefferson aims, with ardent desire, at the presidential chair...."

LETTER FROM WASHINGTON TO JEFFERSON, 1797:

"I regret, deeply regret, the difference in opinions which have arisen, and divided you and another principal officer of the government (Hamilton); and wish, devoutly, there could be an accommodation between you by mutual yieldings. A measure of this sort would produce harmony, and consequent good in our public councils; the contrary will, inevitably, introduce confusion and serious mischiefs; and for what? Because mankind cannot think alike, but would adopt different means to attain the same end. For I will frankly and solemnly declare that I believe the views of both of you (Hamilton and Jefferson) are pure, and well meant; and that experience alone will decide (who is right)...."

THOMAS JEFFERSON'S OPINION OF ALEXANDER HAMILTON MAY 23, 1792:

"The ultimate object of [Hamilton's program] is to prepare the way for a change, from the present republican form of government, to that of a monarchy, of which the English constitution is the model, [and to produce] in the future a king, lords and commons, or whatever else those who direct it may choose...."

LETTER FROM WASHINGTON TO HAMILTON, 1792:

"Differences in political opinion are as unavoidable as, to a certain point, they may, perhaps, be necessary; but it is exceedingly to be regretted that subjects cannot be discussed with temper on the one hand, or decisions submitted to without having the motives (distorted by the other party). Here we find that men of abilities, zealous patriots, having the same general objects in view, and the same upright intentions to prosecute them, will not exercise more charity in deciding on the opinions and actions of one another....having said these things, I would fain (gladly) hope that liberal allowance will be made for the political opinions of each other, and instead of those wounding suspicions, and irritating charges...that there might be mutual forbearances...on all sides. Without these I do not see how the reins of government are to be managed, or how the union of the states can be much longer preserved."

Compare and contrast the political views of Thomas Jefferson and Alexander Hamilton.

How did Washington feel about the political "feuds" of Jefferson and Hamilton?

Chapter Four
The Jeffersonian Era

"Those who labor in the earth are the chosen people of God, if ever he had a chosen people, whose breasts He has made His peculiar deposit for substantial and genuine virtue."——*Thomas Jefferson*

Thomas Jefferson is best remembered as the author of the *Declaration of Independence*. His stirring words in that document not only served to inspire the continuation of the American Revolution, but have served as a guide for subsequent generations of Americans. All men are created equal has become the credo and idea for millions of American citizens. Yet there are many who question the sincerity of the author of these words. Jefferson, who espoused the merits of the yeoman farmer, lived in a grand mansion and spent lavishly. At the time of his death in 1826, Jefferson was over $250,000.00 in debt. (An enormous sum by the standards of the 19th century.) He attempted to introduce an anti-slavery provision into the *Declaration of Independence*, but he owned hundreds of slaves himself. Jefferson was also a man of great sophistication. As a polymath who understood several languages, a trained lawyer who understood the intricacies of debate, an inventor whose own home Monticello stands as a monument to his genius, and the owner of a library that contained over 10,000 books, Jefferson had little in common with the average man.

Perhaps it is more important to look past the seeming contradictions in Jefferson's character and focus on the impact of his actions. While it may be reasonably argued that Jefferson failed to live up to his own creed, his words continue to inspire us. His belief that the future of America would be best served not by the vested interests of the plutocrats, but by the men who earned their living by the sweat of their brow was heartfelt. Additionally, Jefferson understood the importance of providing an education for the average citizen. His rhetoric regarding education would lay the foundations for public education in the United States. The impact of his thinking on American society has been enormous.

Jefferson's presidency also presents us with contradictions. An ardent advocate of states' rights, Jefferson often pursued a path of national interests as presidency most notably, his authorization of the purchase of the Louisiana territory, despite the rather dubious constitutional authority to do so. Jefferson found, as presidents often do, that expediency must at times take precedence over ideology. Students who study the Jeffersonian era might ought to look at the full range of his life before passing judgment.

(Mr. Jefferson's view of government is clearly stated in his first inaugural address delivered in 1801.)

JEFFERSON'S FIRST INAUGURAL ADDRESS (1801)

It is proper you should understand what I deem the essential principles of our government: ...Equal and exact justice to all men, of whatever state or persuasion, religious or political; peace, commerce, and honest friendship with all nations, entangling alliances with none; the support of the state governments in all their rights, as the most competent administrations for our domestic concerns and the surest bulwarks against anti-republican tendencies; the preservation of the general government in its whole constitutional vigor, as the sheet anchor of our peace at home and safety abroad; a jealous care of the right of election by the people....

I know, indeed, that some honest men fear that a Republican government can not be strong, that this Government is not strong enough; but would the honest patriot, in the full tide of successful experiment, abandon a government which has so far kept us free and firm on the theoretic and visionary fear that this Government, the world's best hope, may by possibility want energy to preserve itself? I trust not. I believe this, on the contrary, the strongest Government on earth. I believe it the only one where every man, at the call of the law, would fly to the standard of the law, and would meet invasions of the public order as his own personal concern. Sometimes it is said that man can not be trusted with the government of himself. Can he, then, be trusted with the government of others? Or have we found angels in the forms of kings to govern him? Let history answer this question.

(From Thomas Jefferson, *First Inaugural Address*, 1801)

How would you summarize Jefferson's view of government?

(Under John Adams's, and later during Thomas Jefferson's presidency, political rhetoric came to full force. The election of 1800 was one of the most controversial in American history.)

THE REPUBLICAN VIEW OF THE FEDERALISTS

It is not so well known, as it should be, that this federal gem [John Adams], this apostle of the parsons of Connecticut, is not only a repulsive pedant, a gross hypocrite, and an unprincipled oppressor, but that he is, in private life, one of the most egregious fools upon the continent. When some future Clarendon shall illustrate and dignify the annals of the present age, he will assuredly express his surprise at the abrupt and absurd elevation of this despicable attorney. He will enquire by what species of madness, America submitted to accept, as her president, a person without abilities, and without virtues; a being alike incapable of attracting either tenderness, or esteem. The historian will search for those occult causes that induced her to exalt an individual, who has neither that innocence of sensibility, which incites us to love, nor that omnipotence of intellect which commands us to admire. He will ask why the United States degraded themselves to the choice of a wretch, whose soul came blasted from the hand of nature; of a wretch, that has neither the science of a magistrate, the politeness of a courtier, nor the courage of a man.

(From James T. Callender, *The Prospect before Us*, 1800)

A FEDERALIST VIEW OF REPUBLICANS

The fate of Frenchmen will be the fate of Americans. The French boasted that they were the most civilized and humane people in the world. We can say no more of ourselves. Their Jacobins were wicked, cruel, profligate, atheistical—ours are the same. Their pretence ever was, to consult the good of the people—ours make the same. The people in that country have been robbed, enslaved, and butchered—we shall be served in the same manner, unless we arouse instantly, and rescue our government from the fangs of those who are tearing it in pieces. The struggle will be great, but, if successful on our part, it will also be glorious. Look at your houses, your parents, your wives and your children. Are you prepared to see your dwellings in flames, hoary hairs bathed in blood, female chastity violated, or children riding on the pike and the halberd? If not, prepare for the task of protecting your Government. Look at every leading Jacobin as at a ravening wold, preparing to enter your peaceful fold, and glut his deadly appetite on the vitals of your country. Already do their hearts leap at the prospect. Having long brooded over these scenes of death and despair, they now wake as from a trance, and in imagination seizing the dagger and the musket, prepare for the work of slaughter. GREAT GOD OF COMPASSION AND JUSTICE, SHIELD MY COUNTRY FROM DESTRUCTION.
(From *The Connecticut Courant*, September 29, 1800. Signed "Burleigh.")

Compare the campaign rhetoric of 1800 with that of today.

(Ironically, it was under Jefferson's administration that the Supreme Court began to emerge as a powerful force in American society. As the power of the Supreme Court grew, so did the power of the federal government. The man who strengthened the position of the Supreme Court was John Marshall. In a series of rulings and opinions, the Marshall Court helped form the national union.)

MARBURY V. MADISON (1803)

The powers of the legislature are defined and limited; and that those limits may not be mistaken, or forgotten, the constitution is written. To what purpose are powers limited, and to what purpose is that limitation committed to writing, if these limits may, at any time, be passed by those intended to be restrained?...It is a proposition too plain to be contested that the Constitution controls any legislative act repugnant to it....A legislative act contrary to the Constitution is not law....It is emphatically the province and duty of the judicial department to say what the law is....—United States Supreme Court.

From Marbury v. Madison, (1803)

MCCULLOCH V. MARYLAND (1819)

THE POWER TO TAX involves the power to destroy....If the states may tax one instrument, employed by the [federal] government in the execution of its powers, they may tax any and every other instrument. They may tax the mail; they may tax the mint; they may tax patent rights; they may tax the papers of the customhouse; they may tax judicial process; they may tax all the means employed by the government, to an excess which would defeat all the ends of government. This was not intended by the American people. They did not design to make their government dependent on the states....

The question is, in truth, a question of supremacy; and if the right of the states to tax the means employed by the general government be conceded, the declaration that the Constitution, and the laws made in pursuance thereof, shall be supreme law of the land, is empty and unmeaning declamation....

From McCulloch v. Maryland, 1819

MARSHALL ON INTERPRETING THE CONSTITUTION

[The Constitution] contains an enumeration of powers expressly granted by the people to their government. It has been said that these powers ought to be construed strictly. But why ought they to be so construed? Is there one sentence in the constitution which gives countenance to this rule? In the last of the enumerated powers, that which grants, expressly, the means for carrying all others into execution, congress is authorized "to make all laws which shall be necessary and proper" for the purpose....What do gentlemen mean by a strict construction? If they contend only against that enlarged construction which would extend words beyond their natural and obvious import, we...should not controvert the principle. If they contend for that narrow construction which, in support of some theory not to be found in the constitution, would deny to the government those powers which the words of the grant, as usually understood, import, and which are consistent with the general views and objects of the instruments; for that narrow construction, which would cripple the government, and render it unequal to the objects for which it is declared to be instituted, and to which to the powers given, as fairly understood, render it competent; then we cannot perceive the propriety of this strict construction, nor adopt it as the rule by which the constitution is to be expounded.

From Gibbons v. Ogden, 1824

What was the overall significance of the Marbury v. Madison case of 1803?

How did the Marshall court's ruling in McCulloch v. Maryland strengthen the federal government?

How did John Marshall feel the constitution was to be interpreted?

(The Virginia Dynasty finally ended with the election of John Quincy Adams in 1824. One of the most important documents to come out of the post-Jeffersonian era was the Monroe Doctrine. Issued by President Monroe in 1823, it has served as the cornerstone of American foreign policy ever since.)

MONROE DOCTRINE (1823)

THE AMERICAN CONTINENTS...are henceforth not to be considered as subjects for future colonization by any European powers....We owe it, therefore, to candor and to the amicable relations existing between the United States and those powers [Quadruple Alliance] to declare that we should consider any attempt on their part to extend their system to any portion of this hemisphere as dangerous to our peace and safety. With the existing colonies or dependencies of any European power, we have not interfered and shall not interfere. But with the governments who have declared their independence and maintained it, and whose independence we have...acknowledged, we could not view any interposition for the purpose of oppressing them, or controlling in any other manner their destiny, by any European power in any other light than as the manifestation of an unfriendly disposition toward the United States....

Our policy in regard to Europe, which was adopted at an early stage of the wars which have so long agitated that quarter of the globe, nevertheless remains the same, which is, not to interfere in the internal concerns of any of its powers....

To whom was President Monroe addressing this message?

How has the Monroe Doctrine helped to shape American foreign policy?

Chapter Five
The Jacksonian Era

"One man with courage makes a majority."—*Andrew Jackson*

Andrew Jackson's life encompasses the American experience from 1776 to the onset of Western expansion in the 1840s. As a very young man he served in the revolutionary army. He emerged from near poverty to become a prosperous farmer. His mansion in Nashville, Tennessee, known as the *Hermitage*, is impressive even by the standards of the present time. He earned his military reputation by fighting Indians on the frontier and by his defeat of the British at the Battle of New Orleans in early 1815. Jackson was very much a product of the frontier. He fought several duels and he projected an image of toughness. He was wounded in one of the duels he fought and carried the bullet, lodged in his chest, for the rest of his days. He extended his frontier toughness into the political arena, first in Tennessee politics and then upon the national scene, beginning with his first run for president in 1824.

Jackson's frontier experience caused him to create a political philosophy based upon a belief in the common man. His politics were a radical extension of Jeffersonian democracy. While Jefferson exhorted the yeoman farmer, Jacksonian democracy tended to disregard property ownership as a prerequisite for political participation. Like Jefferson, Jackson mistrusted the ambitions of the commercial entities in America. He was reluctant to expand the power of the federal government to promote the business community, and subsequently vetoed legislation aimed at doing so. Jacksonian political theory embraced states' rights. Self reliance and independence were hallmarks of the Jacksonian creed. The age of Jackson also saw the spread of public education. Education was promoted as a duty of each community to help educate the common citizen for participation in the political process.

Like Jefferson, Jackson found it difficult to hold to all his campaign rhetoric. When South Carolina threatened to secede from the Union over the tariff issue, Jackson was forced to take a decidedly pro-union position. The crisis was averted only after a compromise on the tariff was arrived at. Indeed Jackson's two terms were contentious enough to bring a complete end to the one party system in American politics. Jackson did not see his sometimes arbitrary style of presidential leadership as incongruent with the message of rule by the common man. Jackson believed that the presidency, the only office elected by the majority of the people, was the embodiment of true democracy.

(Andrew Jackson, although far from being an average man himself, considered himself a friend of the average man. Often this meant he had to attack the wealthy as being uninterested in the welfare of the nation as a whole.)

JACKSON ATTACKS THE RICH

It is to be regretted, that the rich and powerful too often bend the acts of government to their selfish purposes. Distinctions in society will always exist under every just government. Equality of talents, or education, or of wealth can not be produced by human institutions. In the full enjoyment of the gifts of Heaven and the fruits of superior industry, economy, and virtue, every man is equally entitled to protection by law; but when the laws undertake to add to these natural and just advantages artificial distinctions...to make the rich richer and the potent more powerful, the humble members of society – the farmers, mechanics, and laborers – who have neither the time nor the means of securing like favors to themselves, have a right to complain of the injustice of their government.

(From a Jackson speech)

What area of the country would have found this speech appealing?

What is the role of the common man in government according to Jackson?

(How did Jacksonian Democracy originate? According to the noted historian Frederick Jackson Turner, it was a result of the frontier experience.)

FREDERICK JACKSON TURNER ON "FRONTIER DEMOCRACY"

Out of the frontier democratic society where the freedom and abundance of land in the great Valley opened a refuge to the oppressed in all religions, came the Jacksonian democracy which governed the nation after the downfall of the party of John Quincy Adams...It was in this same period, and largely by reason of the drainage of population to the West, and the stir in the air raised by the Western winds of Jacksonian democracy, that most of the older States reconstructed their constitutions on a more democratic basis. From the Mississippi Valley where there were liberal suffrage provisions (based on population alone instead of property and population), disregard of vested interest, and insistence on the rights of man, came the inspiration for this era of change in the franchise and apportionment, or reform of laws for imprisonment for debt, of general attacks upon monopoly and privilege. "It is now plain," wrote Jackson in 1837, "that the war is to be carried on by monied aristocracy of the few against the democracy of numbers..."
(Adapted from a Turner speech in 1910)

According to Frederick Jackson Turner, how did the frontier promote democracy?

What criticisms of Turner's view can you think of?

(Jackson was a proponent of states' rights. Yet, he thought the union had to be maintained. He adamantly opposed the concept of nullification.)

JACKSON ON NULLIFICATION

The ordinance is founded...on the strange position that any one State may not only declare an act of Congress void, but prohibit its execution; that the true construction of that instrument permits a State to retain its place in the Union and yet be bound by no other of its laws than those it may choose to consider as constitutional....But reasoning on this subject is superfluous when our social compact, in express terms, declares that the laws of the United States, its Constitution, and treaties made under it are the supreme law of the land, and, for greater caution, adds "that the judges in every State shall be bound thereby, anything in the constitution or laws of any State to the contrary notwithstanding." And it may be asserted without fear of refutation that no federative government could exist without a similar provision....

If the doctrine of a State veto upon the laws of the Union carries with it internal evidence of its impractical absurdity, our constitutional history will also afford abundant proof that it would have been repudiated with indignation had it been proposed to form a feature in our Government....

I consider, then, the power to annul a law of the United States, assumed by one State, incompatible with the existence of the Union, contradicted expressly by the letter of the Constitution, unauthorized by its spirit, inconsistent with every principle on which it was founded, and destructive of the great object for which it was formed.

(From Andrew Jackson, Proclamation to the People of South Carolina, December 10, 1832)

CALHOUN ON THE NATURE OF THE UNION

The great and leading principle is, that the General Government emanated from the people of the United States, forming distinct political communities, and acting in their separate and sovereign capacity, and not from all of the people forming one aggregate political community; that the Constitution of the United States is, in fact, a compact, to which each State is a party, in the character already described; and that the several States, or parties, have a right to judge of its infractions; and in case of a deliberate, palpable, and dangerous exercise of power not delegated, they have the right, in the last resort, to use the language of the Virginia Resolutions, "to interpose for arresting the progress of evil, and for appertaining to them." This right of interposition...be it called what it may—mental principle of our system, resting on facts historically as certain as our revolution itself, and deductions as simple and demonstrative as that of any political or moral truth whatever; and I firmly believe that on its recognition depend that stability and safety of our political institutions.
(From John C. Calhoun, Fort Hill Address, July 26, 1831.)

Define the concept of nullification. Compare and contrast the views on nullification of Jackson and Calhoun.

(As the frontier line moved farther west in the 19ᵗʰ century, white men and red men found themselves vying for the same land. Jackson's solution to the problem was "to remove the problem." The removal of the Five Civilized Tribes to lands farther west is one of the saddest episodes in American history.)

THE REMOVAL OF THE FIVE CIVILIZED TRIBES

"Where the white man puts down his foot, he never takes it up again," is a shrewd and correct remark of an Indian chief. The hunting grounds of the Indians on our frontiers are explored in all directions by enterprising white people. Their best lands are selected, settled, and, at length, purchased by treaty. Their game is either wholly destroyed or so diminished as not to yield adequate support.

The poor Indians, thus deprived of their accustomed means of subsistence, and of what, in their own view, can alone render them respectable as well as comfortable, are constrained to leave their homes, their goodly lands, and the graves of their fathers, and either go into new and less valuable wilderness and mingle with other tribes, dependent on their hospitality for a meager support; or, without the common aids of education, to change at once all their habits and modes of life, remaining on a fraction of the lands they once owned, which they know not how to cultivate and to which they have not a complete title. In these circumstances they become insulated among those who despise them as an inferior race, fit companions only of those who have the capacity and the disposition to corrupt them. In this degraded, most disconsolate, and heart sinking of all situations in which man can be placed, they are left miserably to waste away for a few generations, and then to become extinct forever!

This is no fancied picture. In a few years it will be sad reality unless we change our policy towards them, unless effectual measures are taken to bring them over this awful gulf to the solid and safe ground of civilization. How many tribes, once numerous and respectable, have in succession perished, in the manner described, from their fair and productive territories now possessed by and giving support to TEN MILLIONS OF PEOPLE!...

On the subject of removal of the Indians who now dwell within our settlements, there are different opinions among wise and good men. The point on which they divide is whether it is best to let these Indians quietly remain on their present reservations, and to use our endeavors to civilize them where they are; or for the government to take their reservations and give them an equivalent in lands to be purchased from other tribes beyond our present settlements. The Indians themselves are divided in opinion on this subject. Some are for removing and some for remaining, as in the case of the Cherokees, Delawares, Senecas, Oneidas, Shawnees, and indeed most of the other tribes living among us.

Difficulties in deciding this question present themselves, from whichever side it is viewed. To remove these Indians far away from their present homes, from "the bones of their fathers" into a wilderness among strangers, possibly hostile, to live as their new neighbors live—by hunting, a state to which they have not lately been accustomed and which is incompatible with civilization—can hardly be reconciled with the professed views and objects of the government in civilizing them. This would not be deemed by the world a wise course, not one which would very probably lead to the desired end.

If only those who are willing to go are moved and the others remain—this division of already enfeebled *remnants* of tribes would only still more weaken their strength, diminish their influence, and hasten their destruction. Nor would this partial removal satisfy those who want to remove all the Indians, nor those who want to retain them all. The latter wish them to remain for the benevolent purpose of educating them all where they now are. The Indians, they say, are now among us, in the midst of examples of civilized life, and where necessary instruction can be imparted to them conveniently and with little expense.

On the other hand, there is much to be said in favor of the

removal of the smaller tribes and remnants of tribes—not, however, into the wilderness, to return again to the savage life, but to some suitable prepared portion of our country where, collected in one body, they may be made comfortable and with advantage be educated together, as has already been mentioned, in the manner in which we educate our own children. Some such course as this, I feel, will satisfy a great majority of the reflecting part of those who interest themselves at all in this subject. It is, in my belief, the only practicable course which can be pursued consistently with the professed object of the government.
(Adapted from Jedidiah Morse, *A Report to the Secretary of War of the United States on Indian Affairs*)

What two viewpoints are put forth towards the removal of the Indians?

Was Jackson justified in removing the Indians?

(Not all who observed American democracy during the Jacksonian era were complimentary. In his famous work, "Democracy in America," the Frenchman Alexis De Tocqueville expressed concerns that American democracy could lead to a "tyranny by the majority.")

ALEXIS DE TOCQUEVILLE'S DEMOCRACY IN AMERICA

The very essence of democratic government consists in the absolute sovereignty of the majority;...The moral authority of the majority is partly based upon the notion that there is more intelligence and more wisdom in a great number of men collected together than in a single individual, and that the number of legislators is more important than their quality...[it] is founded upon yet another principle,...that the interests of the many are to be preferred to those of the few...

If it be admitted that a man, possessing absolute power, may misuse that power by wronging his adversaries, why should a majority not be liable to the same reproach? Men are not apt to change their characters by agglomeration...

When an individual or a party is wronged in the United States, to whom can he apply for redress? If to public opinion, public opinion constitutes the majority; if to the legislature, it represents the majority, and implicitly obeys its injunction; if to the executive power, it is appointed by the majority, and remains a passive tool in its hands: the public troops consist of the majority under arms; the jury is the majority invested with the right of hearing judicial cases...However iniquitous or absurd the evil of which you complain may be, you must submit to it as well as you can...

I know no country in which there is so little true independence of mind and freedom of discussion as in America. In any constitutional state in Europe every sort of religious and political theory may be advocated and propagated abroad...But in a nation where democratic institutions exist, organized like those of the United States, there is but one sole authority, one single element of strength and of success, with nothing beyond it. In America, the majority raises very formidable barriers to the liberty of opinion; within these barriers an author may write whatever he pleases, but he will repent it if he ever steps beyond them. Not that he is exposed to the terrors of the auto da fé [burning at the stake], but...his political career is closed forever...every sort of compensation...is refused to him...those who think like him, without having the courage to speak, abandon him in silence.

If ever the free institutions of America are destroyed, that event may be attributed to the unlimited authority of the majority, which may at some future time urge the minorities to desperation, and oblige them to have recourse to physical force. Anarchy will then be the result, but it will have been brought about by despotism.

(Alexis De Tocqueville, *Democracy in America*, 1835.)

What concerns did De Tocqueville have about American democracy?

Why would his European heritage impact his judgment?

Chapter Six
The Literary and Reform Movements

"Equality suggests to the human mind several ideas that would not have originated from any other source, and it modifies almost all those previously entertained."—Alexis De Tocqueville

As the United States approached the mid 19th century it was still seeking a literary identity. The literary movement known as Transcendentalism (1840-1860) emphasized the need for an original form of literature for the United States. The movement was led by Ralph Waldo Emerson of Concord, Massachusetts. The Transcendentalist Movement focused on the concept of self-reliance and produced, perhaps, America's most original thinker, Henry David Thoreau. The movement was heavily influenced by European Romanticism and especially the notion of God being immanent in nature and the human soul.

The Transcendentalist Movement helped to shape American social attitudes relating to self-reliance, abolitionism, feminism, and utopian socialism. As the individual spirit needed liberation according to the transcendentalists, so did society as a whole. It is not surprising to find women leading many of the reform movements of the late 19th century. While not afforded political status themselves, women found their voice in these various reform movements.

(What was distinctively American about the literature produced in these United States in the 19th Century? An answer to the question would be very subjective. By the early 19th Century, American literature had become identified with the American character. The selections below are offered as examples of distinctively American works.)

EMERSON ON MANKIND

The intuition of the moral sentiment is an insight of the perfection of the laws of the soul. These laws execute themselves. Thus in the soul of man there is a justice where retributions are instant and entire. He who does a noble deed is instantly ennobled. He who does a mean deed is by the action itself contracted. He who puts off impurity, thereby puts on purity. If a man is at heart just, then in so far is he God; the safety of God, the immortality of God, the majesty of God do enter into that man with justice.... Good is positive. Evil is merely privative, not absolute: it is like cold, which is the privation of heat. All evil is so much death or nonentity. Benevolence is absolute and real. So much benevolence as a man hath, so much life hath he. For all things proceed out of this same spirit, which is differently named love, justice, temperance, in its different applications.... Whilst a man seeks good ends, he is strong by the whole strength of nature. In so far as he roves from these ends, he bereaves himself of power, or auxiliaries; his being shrinks out of all remote channels, he becomes less and less, a mote, a point, until absolute badness is absolute death.

(From Ralph Waldo Emerson, "Divinity School Address," 1838.)

THOREAU ON INDIVIDUALISM

The authority of government...must have the sanction and consent of the governed. It can have no pure right over my person and property but what I concede to it. The progress from an absolute to a limited monarchy, from a limited monarchy to a democracy, is a progress toward a true respect for the individual. Is a democracy, such as we know it, the last improvement possible in government? Is it not possible to take a step further towards recognizing and organizing the rights of man? There will never be a really free and enlightened State, until the State comes to recognize the individual as a higher and independent power, from which all its own power and authority are derived, and treats him accordingly. I please myself with imagining a State at last which can afford to be just to all men, and to treat the individual with respect as a neighbor; which even would not think it inconsistent with its own repose, if a few were to live aloof from it, not meddling with it, nor embraced by it, who fulfilled all the duties of neighbors and fellowmen. A State which bore this kind of fruit, and suffered it to drop off as fast as it ripened, would prepare the way for a still more perfect and glorious State, which also I have imagined, but not anywhere seen.

(From Henry David Thoreau Essay on *Civil Disobedience*, 1849.)

WHITMAN ON THE AMERICAN GENIUS

The genius of the United States is not best or most in its executives or legislatures, nor in its ambassadors or authors or colleges or churches or parlors, nor even in its newspapers or inventors...but always most in the common people. Their manners, speech, dress, friendships—the freshness and candor of their physiognomy—the picturesque looseness of their carriage...their deathless attachment to freedom—their aversion to anything indecorous or soft or mean—the practical acknowledgement of the citizens of one state by the citizens of all other states—the fierceness of their roused resentment—their curiosity and welcome of novelty—their self-esteem and wonderful sympathy—their susceptibility to a slight—the air they have of persons who never knew how it felt to stand in the presence of superiors—the fluency of their speech—their delight in music, the sure symptom of manly tenderness and native elegance of soul...their good temper and openhandedness—the terrible significance of their elections—the President's taking off his hat to them not they to him—these too are unrhymed poetry. It awaits the gigantic and generous treatment worthy of it.

(From Walt Whitman, Preface to *Leaves of Grass*, 1855.)

Reread each of the passages and consider how the "American experience" would have influenced each author.

(The reform movement, which hit full stride in the 1830's, brought about significant changes in American life. Alexis De Tocqueville had an opinion as to why Americans were so involved with reforms.)

DE TOCQUEVILLE ON AMERICAN REFORM

"Equality suggests to the human mind several ideas that would not have originated from any other source, and it modifies almost all those previously entertained. I take as an example the idea of human perfectibility, because it is one of the principal notions that the intellect can conceive and because it constitutes of itself a great philosophical theory, which is everywhere to be traced by its consequences in the conduct of human affairs.

Although man has many points of resemblance with the brutes, one trait is peculiar to himself: he improves; they are incapable of improvement. Mankind could not fail to discover this difference from the beginning. The idea of perfectibility is therefore as old as the world; equality did not give birth to it, but has imparted to it a new character.

When the citizens of a community are classed according to rank, profession, or birth and when all men are forced to follow the career which chance has opened before them, everyone thinks that the utmost limits of human power are to be discerned in proximity to himself, and no one seeks any longer to resist the inevitable law of his destiny. Not indeed, that an aristocratic people absolutely deny man's faculty of self-improvement, but they do not hold it to be indefinite; they can conceive amelioration, but not change; they imagine that the future condition of society may be better, but not essentially different; and while they admit that humanity has made progress they assign to it beforehand certain impassable limits.

Thus they do not presume that they have arrived at the supreme good or at absolute truth...but they cherish an opinion that they have pretty near reached that degree of greatness and knowledge which our imperfect nature admits of; and as nothing moves about them, they are willing to fancy that everything is in its fit place. Then it is that the legislator affects to lay down eternal laws; that kings and nations will raise none but imperishable monuments; and that the present generation undertakes to spare generations to come of the care of regulating their destinies....

Aristocratic nations are naturally too liable to narrow the scope of human perfectibility; democratic nations, to expand it beyond reason."

According to De Tocqueville, what separates man from brutes?

(Many women were involved in the reform movement of the 19th Century. Ironically, women were still being treated as second-class citizens. The first women's-rights convention in the United States was held at Seneca Falls, New York, in 1848. The Declaration of Sentiments issued at the Seneca Falls convention clearly states the plight of the 19th Century American woman.)

THE SENECA FALLS DECLARATION

When, in the course of human events, it becomes necessary for one portion of the family of man to assume among the people of the earth a position different from that which they have hitherto occupied, but one to which the laws of nature and of nature's God entitle them, a decent respect to the opinions of mankind requires that they should declare the causes that impel them to such a course.

We hold these truths to be self-evident: that all men and women are created equal; that they are endowed...with certain inalienable rights...that to secure these rights governments are instituted, deriving their just powers from the consent of the governed. Whenever any form of government becomes destructive of these ends, it is the right of those who suffer from it to refuse allegiance to it, and to insist upon the institution of a new government....Such has been the patient sufferance of the women under this government, and such is now the necessity which constrains them to demand the equal station to which they are entitled.

The history of mankind is a history of repeated injuries...on the part of man toward woman...

He has compelled her to submit to laws, in the formation of which she had no voice...

He has made her, if married, in the eye of the law, civilly dead.

He has taken from her all right in property, even to wages she earns. He has so framed the laws of divorce, as to what shall be the proper causes, and in case of separation, to whom the guardianship of the children shall be given,...the law...going upon a false supposition of the supremacy of man, and giving all power into his hands.

He has monopolized nearly all the profitable employments, and from those she is permitted to follow, she receives but scanty remuneration. As a teacher of theology, medicine, or law, she does not know.

He has denied her the facilities for obtaining a thorough education, all colleges being closed against her.

He allows her in Church, as well as State, but in a subordinated position, claiming Apostolic authority for her exclusion from the ministry, and with some exceptions, from any public participation in the affairs of the Church...

What were the complaints of the women at Seneca Falls?

Chapter Seven
Manifest Destiny and the Slavery Issue

"We must ever maintain the principle that the people of this continent alone have the right to decide their own destiny."—*Senator Corwin*

By the 1840's virtually all of the United States east to the Mississippi river had been settled. The movement west of the Mississippi was encouraged by the popular press of the time and eventually by the United States government itself. The annexation of Texas in the 1840s and the passage of the Homestead Act in 1862, gave impetus to the westward expansion. The right of the American populace to these lands at the expense of Native Americans and other indigenous groups became wrapped up in a concept known as *manifest destiny*. Manifest destiny stated that it was the God-given right of Americans to control all of the continental United States. Minority groups were incidental to this right.

Expansion, however, had its pitfalls. How would the new territory added to the United States be treated in regards to slavery? The slavery question which Thomas Jefferson had referred to as, "*a firebell in the night,*" now threatened to destroy the very ties that bound the United States together. By 1861 good men and the spirit of compromise were unable to hold the nation together as America lapsed into Civil War.

(Not everyone agreed that America had a right to expand her borders. Below are two views on the expansion issue.)

SENATOR CORWIN ON EXPANSION:

"Look at this pretense of want of room. With twenty millions of people, you have about one thousand millions of acres of land, inviting settlement by every conceivable argument.... Why, says the chairman of this Committee on Foreign Relations, it is the most reasonable thing in the world! We ought to have the Bay of San Francisco. Why? Because it is the best harbor on the Pacific! It has been my fortune...to have practiced a good deal in criminal courts in the course of my life, but have never yet heard a thief, arraigned for stealing a horse, plead that it was the best horse that he could find in the country...You still say you want room for your people. This has been the plea of every robber chief from Nimrod to the present hour...."

PRESIDENT POLK ON EXPANSION:

"We must ever maintain the principle that the people of this continent alone have the right to decide their own destiny. (It is) my duty to assert and maintain by all constitutional means the right of the United States to that portion of our territory which lies beyond the Rocky Mountains...Eighty years ago our population was confined on the west by the ridge of the Alleghanies....our people, increasing to many millions, have filled the eastern valley of the Mississippi, adventurously ascended the Missouri to its headsprings and are already engaged in establishing the blessings of self-government in valleys of which the rivers flow to the Pacific....To us belongs the duty of protecting them adequately wherever they may be upon our soil."

On what grounds did Senator Corwin oppose manifest destiny?

How does President Polk justify it?

(The Mexican war would bring vast amounts of territory into the United States. During the war, David Wilmot from Pennsylvania presented his solution to the slavery issue to Congress.)

THE WILMOT PROVISO

"(The) issue now presented is not whether slavery shall exist unmolested where it now is, but whether it shall be carried to new and distant regions, now free, where the footprint of a slave cannot be found. This, sir, is the issue. Upon it I take my stand, and from it I cannot be frightened or driven by the idle charges of abolitionism....I ask not that slavery be abolished. I demand that this government preserve the integrity of free territory against the aggressions of slavery—against its wrongful usurpations....We are told that California is ours, that New Mexico is ours—won by the valor of our arms. They are free. Shall they remain free? Shall these fair provinces be the inheritance and homes of the white labor of freemen or the black labor of slaves? This, sir, is the issue...."

(From David Wilmont's proposal to Congress)

(In the late 1850s, Stephen Douglas, from Illinois, proposed his solution to the slavery issue. His solution was a concept known as "popular sovereignty.")

POPULAR SOVEREIGNTY

"In my opinion, our government can endure forever, divided into free and slave states as our fathers made it.

Each state has the right to prohibit, abolish or sustain slavery, just as it pleases. This government was made upon the great basis of the sovereignty of the states, with each state having the right to regulate its own domestic institutions to suit itself...For this reason this union was established on the right of each state to do as it pleased...to adapt to its conditions and wants...on the question of slavery and every other question. The various states were not allowed to complain of, much less interfere with, the policy of its neighbors....I say to you that there is but one hope, one safety, for this country, and that is to stand immovable by that principle which declares the right of each state and each territory to decide these questions for themselves...."

Which of these "solutions" was more practical?

The slavery issue produced varying viewpoints on the subject. Not only abolitionists and slaves were brought into the debate, but politicians as well. The most famous political debates on the issue were between Abraham Lincoln and Stephen Douglas, during the senate race in Illinois in 1858.

A PRO-SLAVERY VIEW

The negro slaves of the South are the happiest, and, in some sense, the freest people in the world. The children and the aged and infirm work not at all, and yet have all the comforts and necessaries of life provided for them. They enjoy liberty, because they are oppressed neither by care or labor. The women do little hard work, and are protected from the despotism of their husbands by their masters. The negro men and stout boys work, on the average, in good weather, not more than nine hours a day...Besides, they have their Sabbaths and holidays. White men, with so much of license and liberty, would die of ennui; but negroes luxuriate in corporeal and mental repose. With their faces 'upturned to the sun, they can sleep at any hour; and quiet sleep is the greatest of human enjoyments....The free laborer must work or starve. He is more of a slave than the negro, because he works longer and harder for less allowance than the slave, and has no holiday, because the cares of life with him begin when its labors end. He has no liberty, and not a single right.

(From George Fitzhugh, *Cannibals All!*, 1857.)

AN ABOLITIONIST VIEW

The slave is held simply for the use of his master, to whose behests his life, liberty, and happiness are devoted, and by whom he may be bartered, leased, mortgaged, bequeathed, invoiced, shipped as cargo, stored as goods, sold on execution, [and] knocked off at public auction...all according to law. Nor is there anything, within the limit of life, inflicted on a beast, which may not be inflicted on the slave. He may be marked like a hog, branded like a mule, yoked like an ox, hobbled like a horse, driven like an ass, sheared like a sheep, maimed like a cur, and constantly beaten like a brute,—all according to law. And should life itself be taken, what is the remedy? The Law of Slavery...openly pronounces the incompetency of the whole African race, whether bond or free, to testify against a white man in any case, and thus, after surrendering the slave to all possible outrage, crowns its tyranny by excluding the very testimony through which the bloody cruelty of the Slave-Master might be exposed....

...Unhappily, there is Barbarism elsewhere in the world; but American Slavery, as defined by existing law, stands forth as the greatest organized Barbarism on which the sun now looks.

(From Charles Sumner, Speech in the United States Senate, June 4, 1860.)

LINCOLN ON THE SLAVERY QUESTION

I have stated upon former occasions...what I understand to be the real issue in this controversy between Judge Douglas and myself. On the point of my wanting to make war between the Free and the Slave States, there has been no issue between us. So, too, when he assumes that I am in favor of introducing a perfect social and political equality between the white and black races. These are false issues....The real issue in this controversy—the one pressing upon every mind—is the sentiment on the part of one class that looks upon the institution of slavery as a wrong, and of another class that does not look upon it as a wrong. The sentiment that contemplates the institution of slavery in this country as a wrong, is the sentiment of the Republican party.... They look upon it as being a moral, social, and political wrong; and while they contemplate it as such, they nevertheless have due regard for...the difficulties of getting rid of it in any satisfactory way and to all the constitutional obligations thrown about it. Yet...they insist that it should, as far as may be, be treated as a wrong; and one of the methods of treating it as a wrong is to make provision that it shall grow no larger.
(From Abraham Lincoln, Speech at Alton, Illinois, October 15, 1858.)

DOUGLAS ON THE SLAVERY QUESTION

We ought to extend to the negro race...all the rights, all the privileges, and all the immunities which they can exercise consistently with the safety of society. Humanity requires that we should give them all these privileges; Christianity commands that we should extend those privileges to them. The question then arises, What are those privileges, and what is the nature and extent of them? My answer is, that is a question which each State must answer for itself.... If the people of all the States will act on that great principle, and each State mind its own business, attend to its own affairs, take care of its own negroes, and not meddle with its neighbors, then there will be peace between the North and the South, the East and the West, throughout the whole Union.

Why can we not thus have peace?...The moment the North obtained the majority in the House and Senate by admission of California, and could elect a President without the aid of Southern votes, that moment ambitious Northern men formed a scheme to excite the North against the South, and make the people be governed in their votes by geographical lines, thinking that the North, being the stronger section, would outvote the South, and consequently they, the leaders, would ride into office on a sectional hobby.

(From Stephen A. Douglas, Speech at Alton, Illinois, October 15, 1858)

Compare the various views on slavery. What factors would have helped to shape your views on slavery, had you lived during the mid-nineteenth century?

(Perhaps no viewpoint on slavery was as influential as those expressed by Harriet Beecher Stowe in her book, Uncle Tom's Cabin. The book was a national best-seller, and was read widely in European circles.)

UNCLE TOM'S CABIN

"...Legree shook with anger; his greenish eyes glared fiercely. "Here, you rascal, you make believe to be so pious—didn't you never hear out of yer Bible: "Servants, obey yer masters."? Ain't I yer master? Didn't I pay down $1,200 cash for all there is inside your cussed black shell? Ain't you mine, now, body and soul? he said, giving Tom a violent kick with his heavy boot. 'Tell me!'

In the very deep of...suffering...this question shot a gleam of joy and triumph through Tom's soul. He suddenly stretched himself up and, looking to heaven while tears and blood that flowed down his face mingled, he exclaimed, 'no, no! no! My soul ain't yours....You can't harm me....

'I can't', said Legree, with a sneer. 'we'll see...we'll see.'"
(From *Uncle Tom's Cabin*, 1852.)

How would Northerners have reacted to Stowe's book?

Southerners?

Chapter Eight
Civil War and Reconstruction

"...that we here highly resolve that these dead shall not have died in vain; that this nation, under God, shall have a new birth of freedom; and that the government of the people, by the people, for the people, shall not perish from the earth."—Abraham Lincoln

The American Civil War (1861-1865) cost over 600,000 American lives. The destruction of American lives and property continues to impact American society. Many questions relating to the war are still being debated. Was Lincoln responsible for this debacle, or does the blame lie squarely on the shoulders of the aristocracy of the South? Was compromise possible or even desired by 1861? Did the war truly serve to liberate the slave population of the United States? These are all legitimate questions for students of the Civil War to consider.

The Civil War did not solve all the problems that faced the United States. The period after the war usually referred to as the Reconstruction era was one of the bitterest periods in American history. Failure to find suitable answers to the questions relating to the Freedman and the admission of the Southern states into the Union once again, created rifts which still affect the American political landscape.

(When Lincoln was elected president in November of 1860, it was the last straw for many Southerners. In December, 1860, South Carolina seceded from the union. Mr. Lincoln committed his inaugural address on March 4, 1861, to the issue of Civil War.)

SOUTH CAROLINA SECEDES

"We, the people of the State of South Carolina, in convention assembled, do declare and ordain that the union now subsisting between South Carolina and other States under the name of 'The United States of America' is hereby dissolved."

MR. LINCOLN'S FIRST INAUGURAL ADDRESS

"Apprehension seems to exist among the people of the Southern states that their property and their peace and personal security are to be endangered. There has never been any reasonable cause for such apprehension. Indeed, the most ample evidence to the contrary has all the while existed. It is found in nearly all the published speeches of him who now addresses you. I do but quote from one of those speeches when I declare that 'I have no purpose, directly or indirectly, to interfere with the institution of slavery in the states where it exists. I believe I have no lawful right to do so, and I have no inclination to do so.'

In your hands, my dissatisfied fellow countrymen, and not mine, is the momentous issue of civil war. The government will not assail you. You can have no conflict, without being yourselves the aggressors. You have no oath registered in Heaven to destroy the government, while I have the most solemn one to 'preserve, protect, and defend' it.

We are not enemies but friends. We must not be enemies. Though passion may have strained, it must not break our bonds of affection. The mystic chords of memory, stretching from every battlefield and patriot grave, to every living heart and hearth-stone, all over the broad land will yet swell the chorus of the Union, when again touch, as surely they will, the better angels of our nature."

What are Lincoln's comments on the slavery issue?

How is he addressing the Southern states?

Following the momentous battle of Antietam, President Lincoln issued the Emancipation Proclamation of 1863.

LINCOLN TO HIS CABINET ON EMANCIPATION

I have...thought a great deal about the relation of this war to Slavery: and...several weeks ago, I read to you an Order I had prepared on this subject....I have thought...that the time for acting on it might very probably come. I think the time has come now. I wish it were a better time.... The action of the army against the rebels has not been quite what I should have best liked. But they have been driven out of Maryland, and Pennsylvania is no longer in danger of invasion. When the rebel army was at Frederick, I determined, as soon as it should be driven out of Maryland, to issue a Proclamation of Emancipation.... I made the promise to myself, and...to my Maker.... I am going to fulfill that promise.... I do not wish your advice about the main matter.... What I have written is that which my reflections have determined me to say.... I know very well that many others might, in this matter, as in others, do better than I can; and if I were satisfied that the public confidence was more fully possessed by any one of them than by me, and knew of any Constitutional way in which he could be put in my place, he should have it....But though I believe that I have not so much of the confidence of the people as I had some time since, I do not know that...any other person has more; and...I am here. I must do the best I can and bear the responsibility of taking the course which I feel I ought to take.

(From the Diary of Salmon P. Chase, September 22, 1862.)

BOOKER T. WASHINGTON ON THE ATTAINMENT OF FREEDOM

Finally the war closed, and the day of freedom came. It was a momentous and eventful day to all upon our plantation. We had been expecting it. Freedom was in the air, and had been for months....As the great day drew nearer, there was more singing in the slave quarters than usual. It was bolder, had more ring, and lasted later into the night. Most of the verses of the plantation songs had some reference to freedom. True, they had sung those same verses before, but they had been careful to explain that the 'freedom' in those songs referred to the next world, and had no connection with life in this world. Now they gradually threw off the mask....The most distinct thing that I now recall in connection with the scene was that some man who seemed to be a stranger (a United States officer, I presume) made a little speech and then read a rather long paper—the Emancipation Proclamation, I think. After the reading we were told that were all free, and could go when and where we pleased....

For some minutes there was great rejoicing, and thanksgiving, and wild scenes of ecstasy. But there was no feeling of bitterness. [Then suddenly] there was a change in their feelings. The great responsibility of being free, of having charge of themselves...seemed to take possession of them....[W]ithin a few hours the wild rejoicing ceased and a feeling of deep gloom seemed to pervade the slave quarters. To some it seemed that, now that they were in actual possession of it, freedom was a more serious thing than they had expected to find it."
(From a speech by Booker T. Washington)

Explain how the following groups would have reacted to the Emancipation Proclamation:

Northern abolitionists;
Northern soldiers;
Southerners;
Europeans;
The border states.

(In 1863 Mr. Lincoln was asked to "...deliver a few appropriate remarks" at the dedication of the Gettysburg Cemetery. At Gettysburg he delivered one of the most eloquent descriptions of democracy in American history.)

LINCOLN'S GETTYSBURG ADDRESS (1863)

Four score and seven years ago our fathers brought forth on this continent a new nation, conceived in liberty, and dedicated to the proposition that all men are created equal.

Now we are engaged in a great civil war, testing whether that nation, or any nation so conceived and so dedicated, can long endure. We are met on a great battlefield of that war. We have come to dedicate a portion of that field as a final resting place for those who here gave their lives that that nation might live. It is altogether fitting and proper that we should do this.

But, in a larger sense, we cannot dedicate—we cannot consecrate—we cannot hallow—this ground. The brave men, living and dead, who struggled here, have consecrated it far above our poor power to add or detract. [The world will little note nor long remember what we say here, but it can never forget what they did here.] It is for us, the living, rather, to be dedicated here to the unfinished work which they who fought here have thus far so nobly advanced. It is rather for us to be here dedicated to the great task remaining before us—that from these honored dead we take increased devotion to that cause for which they gave the last full measure of devotion; that we here highly resolve that these dead shall not have died in vain; that this nation, under God, shall have a new birth of freedom; and that government of the people, by the people, for the people, shall not perish from the earth.

What do you think are the most important points in Lincoln's Gettysburg Address?

(As the Civil War was winding down, Mr. Lincoln was elected to a second term as president. In his Second Inaugural Address he entertained the prospect of a united nation once again.)

LINCOLN'S SECOND INAUGURAL ADDRESS

...The Almighty has His own purposes. "Woe unto the world because of offences! for it must needs be that offences come; but woe to that man by whom the offence cometh!" If we shall suppose that American Slavery is one of those offences which, in the providence of God, must needs come, but which, having continued through His appointed time, He now wills to remove, and that He gives to both North and South, this terrible war, as the woe due to those by whom the offence came, shall we discern therein any departure from those divine attributes which the believers in a Living God always ascribe to Him? Fondly do we hope—fervently do we pray—that this mighty scourge of war may speedily pass away. Yet, if God wills that it continue, until all the wealth piled by the bond-man's two hundred and fifty years of unrequited toil shall be sunk, and until every drop of blood drawn with the lash, shall be paid by another drawn with the sword, as was said three thousand years ago, so still it must be said "the judgments of the Lord, are true and righteous altogether."

With malice toward none; with charity for all; with firmness in the right, as God gives us to see the right, let us strive on to finish the work we are in; to bind up the nation's wounds; to care for him who shall have borne the battle, and for his widow, and his orphan—to do all which may achieve and cherish a just and a lasting peace, among ourselves, and with all nations.
(From Abraham Lincoln, Inaugural Address, March 4, 1865,)

What was Mr. Lincoln's attitude toward the South in 1865?

(After Mr. Lincoln's assassination in April of 1865, the task of reconstructing the nation fell upon Andrew Johnson and the congress. The Radicals in congress soon found themselves at odds with Mr. Johnson.)

THE RADICAL PLAN OF RECONSTRUCTION

It is the opinion of your committee—

I. That the States lately in rebellion were, at the close of the war, disorganized communities, without civil government, and without constitutions or other forms, by virtue of which political relations could legally exist between them and the federal government.

II. That Congress cannot be expected to recognize as valid the election of representatives from disorganized communities, which, from the very nature of the case, were unable to present their claim to representation under those established and recognized rules, the observance of which has been hitherto required.

III.   That Congress would not be justified in admitting such communities to a participation in the government of the country without first providing such constitutional or other guarantees as will tend to secure the civil rights of all citizens of the republic; a just equality of representation; protection against claims founded in rebellion and crime; a temporary restoration of the right of suffrage to those who had not actively participated in the efforts to destroy the Union and overthrow the government, and the exclusion from positions of public trust of, at least, a portion of those whose crimes have proved them to be enemies to the Union, and unworthy of public confidence.

(From the Report of the Joint Committee on Reconstruction, 1866.)

JOHNSON'S VETO OF THE RADICAL PLAN

The power...given to the commanding officer over all the people of each district is that of an absolute monarch. His mere will is to take the place of all law. The law of the States is now the only rule applicable to the subjects placed under his control, and that is completely displaced by the clause which declares all interference of State authority to be null and void....

It is plain that the authority here given to the military officer amounts to absolute despotism. But to make it more unendurable, the bill provides that it may be delegated to as many subordinates as he chooses to appoint, for it declares that he shall "punish or cause to be punished." Such a power has not been wielded by any monarch in England for more than five hundred years. In all that time no people who speak the English language have borne such servitude. It reduces the whole population of the ten States—all persons, of every color, sex, and condition, and every stranger within their limits—to the most abject and degrading slavery.

(From Andrew Johnson, Veto of the Reconstruction Act, 1867.)

Why did Andrew Johnson oppose the Radical's plan for reconstruction?

Chapter Nine
The Settlement of the West and Industrial Development

"To the frontier the American intellect owes its striking characteristics."—Frederick Jackson Turner

In 1862 the Congress passed the Homestead Act. Lands west of the Mississippi were made available in 160 acre tracts to those who would stay on the land and make improvements for a period of five years. Often these improvements were little more than a wood shack or a sod house. Settlement to the west had begun almost two decades before, but with the Homestead Act the Great Plains was to be settled very rapidly. By 1890 the western frontier was declared settled and there were no more free lands to be had. Perhaps no period in the history of the United States has captured the American imagination as this period has.

As the west was being settled, the nation was involved in a great Civil War (1861-1865). The Civil War helped to launch an unprecedented business boom in America. The period between 1860 and 1890 saw the enormous expansion of American business, the proliferation of railroad lines, and a gradual movement of the American populace into the city. When the transcontinental railroad was finished at Ogden, Utah in 1869, America was linked and forever changed.

TURNER ON THE FRONTIER

To the frontier the American intellect owes its striking characteristics. That coarseness and strength combined with acuteness and inquisitiveness; that practical, inventive turn of mind, quick to find expedients; that masterful grasp of material things, lacking in the artistic but powerful to effect great ends; that restless, nervous energy; that dominant individualism, working for good and for evil, and with all that buoyancy and exuberance which comes with freedom—these are traits of the frontier, or traits called out elsewhere because of the existence of the frontier. Since the days when the fleet of Columbus sailed into the waters of the New World, America has been another name for opportunity, and the people of the United States have taken their tone from the incessant expansion which has not only been open but has even been forced upon them. He would be a rash prophet who should assert that the expansive character of American life has now entirely ceased. Movement has been its dominant fact, and, unless this training has no effect upon a people, the American energy will continually demand a wider field for its exercise. But never again will such gifts of free land offer themselves. (From Frederick Jackson Turner, *The Significance of the Frontier in American History*, 1893.)

According to Turner, how did the frontier serve as an innovator in American history?

(Although not a serious impediment to white settlement, the Indian was seen as a problem. Atrocities were committed by both whites and Indians. The Sand Creek Massacre of 1864 in many ways symbolizes the violence and senselessness of the Indian wars.)

THE SAND CREEK MASSACRE

Lieutenant Cramer Sworn: I am stationed at this post, 1st lieutenant, Company C; veteran battalion, Colorado Cavalry. I was at this post when Colonel Chivington arrived here, and accompanied him on his expedition. He came into the post with a few officers and men, and threw out pickets [guards], with instructions to allow no one to go beyond the line, I was then in command of company K. He brought some eight or nine hundred men with him, and took from this post over a hundred men, all being mounted. My company was ordered along to take part.

We arrived at the Indian village about daylight. On arriving in sight of the village a battalion of the 1st cavalry and the Fort Lyon battalion were ordered on a charge to surround the village and the Indian herd. After driving the herd towards the village, Lieutenant Wilson's battalion of the 1st took possession of the northeast side of the village, Major Anthony's battalion took position on the south, Colonel Chivington's 3rd regiment took position in our rear, dismounted, and after the fight had been commenced by Major Anthony and Lieutenant Wilson, mounted, and commenced firing through us and over our heads. About this time Captain John Smith, Indian interpreter, attempting to come to our troops, was fired on by our men, at the command of some one in our rear, "To shoot the damned old son of a bitch." One of my men rode forward to save him, but was killed. To get out of the fire from the rear, we were ordered to the left.

About this time Colonel Chivington moved his regiment to the front, the Indians retreating up the creek, and hiding under the banks. There seemed to be no organization among our troops; every one on his own hook, and shots flying between our ranks. White Antelope ran towards our columns unarmed, and with both arms raised, but was killed. Several other of the warriors were killed in like manner. The women and children were huddled together, and most of our fire was concentrated on them. Sometimes during the engagement I was compelled to move my company to get out of the fire of our own men. Captain Soule did not order his men to fire when the order was given to commence the fight. During the fight, the battery on the opposite side of the creek kept firing at the bank while our men were in range.

The Indian warriors, about one hundred in number, fought desperately; there were about five hundred all told. I estimated the loss of the Indians to be from one hundred and twenty-five to one hundred and seventy-five killed; no wounded fell into our hands, and all the dead were scalped. The Indian who was pointed out as White Antelope had his fingers cut off....They did not return the fire until after our troops had fired several rounds. We had the assurance from Major Anthony that Black Kettle and his friends should be saved, and only those Indians who had committed depredations should be harmed....Left Hand stood with his arms folded, saying he would not fight the white men, as they were his friends.

I told Colonel Chivington of the position in which the officers stood from Major Wynkoop's pledges to the Indians, and also Major Anthony's, and that it would be murder, in every sense of the word, if he attacked those Indians. His reply was, bringing his fist down close to my face, "Damn any man who sympathizes with Indians." I told him what pledges were given the Indians. He replied, "That he had come to kill Indians, and believed it to be honorable to kill Indians under any and all circumstances." (All this took place at Fort Lyon.) Lieutenant Dunn went to Colonel Chivington and wanted to know if he could kill his prisoner, young Smith. His reply was, "Don't ask me; you know my orders; I want no prisoners." Colonel Chivington was in position where he must have seen the scalping and mutilation going on. One of the soldiers was taking a squaw prisoner across the creek, when other soldiers fired on him, telling him they would kill him if he did not let her go.

On our approach to the village I saw some one with a white flag approaching our lines, and the troops fired upon it; and at the time Captain Smith was fired upon, some one wearing a uniform coat was fired on approaching our lines. Captain Smith was wearing one. After the first I saw the United States flag in the Indian camp. It is a mistake that there were any white scalps found in the village. I saw one, but it was very old, the hair being much faded. I was ordered to burn the village, and was through all the lodges. There was not any snow on the ground, and no rifle-pits.

(*Reports of the Committees of the Senate*, 39th Congress, 2nd Session, No. 156.)

Were the attacks on the Indians at Sand Creek in any way justified?

Mark Twain dubbed the period of industrial growth after the Civil War as the Gilded Age. He was referring to the tremendous wealth that had been created during this period. While Twain and others were very cynical about this era, the wealthy were forced to justify it. In his Gospel of Wealth, Andrew Carnegie speaks of the duties of wealth.)

CARNEGIE'S *GOSPEL OF WEALTH*

This, then, is held to be the duty of the man of wealth: To set an example of modest, unostentatious living, shunning display of extravagance; to provide moderately for the legitimate wants of those dependent upon him; and, after doing so, to consider all surplus revenues which come to him simply as trust funds, which he is called upon to administer, and strictly bound as a matter of duty to administer in the manner which, in his judgment, is best calculated to produce the most beneficial results for the community—the man of wealth thus becoming the mere trustee and agent for his poorer brethren, bringing to their service his superior wisdom, experience, and ability to administer, doing for them better than they would or could do for themselves.

(From Andrew Carnegie, *The Gospel of Wealth and Other Essays*, 1901.)

According to Carnegie, what are the responsibilities of a wealthy man?

(The Gilded Age was marked by widespread corruption in government. The Grant administration was marred by several political scandals. In December of 1876, President Grant apologized for these mistakes.)

PRESIDENT GRANT TO THE CONGRESS IN 1876

Executive Mansion, December 5, 1876.
To the Senate and House of Representatives:

In submitting my eighth and last annual message to Congress it seems proper that I should refer to and in some degree recapitulate the events and official acts of the past eight years.

It was my fortune, or misfortune, to be called to the office of Chief Executive without any previous political training. From the age of 17 I had never even witnessed the excitement attending a Presidential campaign but twice antecedent to my own candidacy, and at but one of them was I eligible as a voter.

Under such circumstances it is but reasonable to suppose that errors of judgment must have occurred. Even had they not, differences of opinion between the Executive, bound by an oath to the strict performance of his duties, and writers and debaters must have arisen. It is not necessarily evidence of blunder on the part of the Executive because there are these differences of views. Mistakes have been made, as all can see and I admit, but it seems to me oftener in the selections made of the assistants appointed to aid in carrying out the various duties of administering the Government—in nearly every case selected without a personal acquaintance with the appointee, but upon recommendations of the representatives chosen directly by the people. It is impossible, where so many trusts are to be allotted, that the right parties should be chosen in every instance. History shows that no Administration from the time of Washington to the present has been free from these mistakes. But I leave comparisons to history, claiming only that I have acted in every instance from a conscientious desire to do what was right, constitutional, within the law, and for the very best interests of the whole people. Failures have been errors of judgment, not of intent....

Did Grant take full responsibility for the problems of his administration? Should he have?

(Life in the cities was harsh for those who had little money. In How the Other Half Lives, Jacob Riis described life in the slums.)

HOW THE OTHER HALF LIVES

...Hamilton Street, like Water Street, is not what it was. The missions drove from the latter the worst of its dives. A sailors' mission has lately made its appearance in Hamilton Street, but there are no dives there, nothing worse than the ubiquitous [everywhere present] saloon and tough tenements.

Enough of them [tenements] everywhere. Suppose we look into one. No. Cherry Street. Be a little careful, please! The hall is dark and you might stumble over the children pitching pennies back there. Not that it would hurt them; kicks and cuffs are their daily diet. They have little else. Here, where the hall turns and dives into utter darkness, is a step, and another, another. A flight of stairs. You can feel your way if you cannot see it. Close? Yes! What would you have? All the fresh air that ever enters these stairs comes from the hall door that is forever slamming, and from the windows of dark bedrooms that in turn receive from the stairs their sole supply of the elements God meant to be free, but man deals out with such niggardly [stingy] hand. That was a woman filling her pail by the hydrant you just bumped against. The sinks are in the hallway, that all the tenants may have access—and all be poisoned alike by their summer stenches. Hear the pump squeak! It is the lullaby of tenement-house babes. In summer, when a thousand thirsty throats pant for a cooling drink in this block, it is worked in vain. But the saloon, whose open door you passed in the hall, is always there. The smell of it has followed you up. Here is a door. Listen! That short hacking cough, that tiny, helpless wail—what do they mean? They mean that the soiled bow of white you saw on the door downstairs will have another story to tell—oh, a sadly familiar story—before the day is at an end. The child is dying with measles. With half a chance it might have lived; but it had none. That dark bedroom killed it.

"It was took all of a suddint," says the mother, smoothing the throbbing little body with trembling hands. There is no unkindness in the rough voice of the man in the jumper, who sits by the window grimly smoking a clay pipe, with the little life ebbing out in his sight, bitter as his words sound: "Hush, Mary! If we cannot keep the baby, need we complain—such as we?

Such as we! What if the words ring in your ears as we grope our way up the stairs and down from floor to floor, listening to the sounds behind the closed doors—some of quarreling, some of coarse songs, more of profanity. They are true. When the summer heats come with their suffering, they have meaning more terrible than words can tell. Come over here. Step carefully over this baby—it is a baby, spite of its rags and dirt—under these iron bridges called fire escapes, but loaded down, despite the incessant watchfulness of the firemen, with broken household goods, with washtubs and barrels, over which no man could climb from a fire. This gap between dingy brick walls is the yard. That strip of smoke-colored sky up there is the heaven of these people. Do you wonder the name does not attract them to the churches? That baby's parents live in the rear tenement here. She is at least as clean as the steps we are now climbing. There are plenty of houses with half a hundred such in. The tenement is much like the one in front we just left, only fouler, closer, darker—we will not say more cheerless. The word is a mockery. A hundred thousand people lived in rear tenements in New York last year [1889]....

What sort of an answer, think you, would come from these tenements to the question, "Is life worth living?" Were they heard at all in the discussion? It may be that this, cut from the last report but one of the Association for the Improvement of the Condition of the Poor, a long name for a weary task, has a suggestion of it: "In the depth of winter the attention of the Association was called to a Protestant family living in a garret in a miserable tenement in Cherry Street. The family's condition was most deplorable, the man, his wife, and three small children shivering in one room through the roof of which the pitiless winds of winter whistled. The room was almost barren of furniture; the parents slept on the floor, the elder children in boxes, and the baby was swung in an old shawl attached to the rafters by cords by way of a hammock. The father, a seaman, had been obliged to give up that calling because he was in consumption [suffered from tuberculosis], and was unable to provide either bread or fire for his little ones."...

(Source: Jacob Riis, *How the Other Half Lives*, New York: Charles Scribner's Sons, 1890.)

(As the giant monopolies gained in power, the working man increased his demands for a better work place. The conflict between labor and big business was long and often violent struggle. Mitchell, in his book on organized labor, states a case for labor.)

WHY LABOR UNIONS ARE NECESSARY

In its fundamental principle trade unionism is plain and clear and simple. Trade unionism starts for the recognition of the fact that under normal conditions the individual, unorganized workman cannot bargain advantageously with the employer for the sale of his labor. Since the workingman has no money in reserve and must sell his labor immediately; since, moreover, he has no knowledge of the market and no skill in bargaining; since, finally, he has only his own labor to see, while the employer engages hundreds of thousands of men and can easily do without the services of any particular individual, the workingman, if bargaining on his own account and for himself alone, is at an enormous disadvantage.

Trade unionism recognizes the fact that under such conditions labor becomes more and more degenerate, because the labor which the workman sells is, unlike other commodities, a thing which is of his very life and soul and being. In the individual contract between a rich employer and a poor workman, the laborer will secure the worst of it; he is progressively debased, because of wages insufficient to buy nourishing food, because of hours of labor too long to permit sufficient rest, because of conditions of work destructive of moral, mental, and physical health, and degrading and annihilating to the laboring classes of the present and the future, and, finally, because of danger from accident and disease, which kill off the workingman or prematurely age him!

(From John Mitchell's, *Organized Labor*, 1903.)

Why did big business oppose the labor movement?

Why did John Mitchell feel unions were necessary?

(The farmers were among the first to speak out against big business. The railroads were their main target. The farmers' movement developed into a quasi-union effort, known as the Grange movement. This movement was instrumental in bringing about government regulation of the railroads.)

THE FARMER'S SIDE (1891)

In the beginning of our history nearly all the people were farmers, and they made our laws; but as the national wealth increased, they gradually dropped out and became hewers of wood and drawers of water to those that own or control large aggregations of wealth. They toiled while others reaped the harvest. It is avarice that despoiled the farmer. Usury absorbed his substance. He sweat gold, and the money changers coined it.

And now, when misfortunes gather about and calamity overtakes him, he appeals to those he has enriched only to learn how poor and helpless he is alone....

From this array of testimony the reader need have no difficulty in determining for himself "how we got here." The hand of the money changer is upon us. Money dictates our financial policy; money controls the business of the country; money is despoiling the people....These men of Wall Street...hold the bonds of nearly every state, county, city, and township in the Union; every railroad owes them more than it is worth. Corners in grain and other products of toil are the legitimate fruits of Wall Street methods. Every trust and combine made to rob the people had its origin in the example of Wall Street dealers....This dangerous power which money gives is fast undermining the liberties of the people. It now has control of nearly half their homes, and is reaching out its clutching hands for the rest. This is the power we have to deal with.

(From John Peffer's, *The Farmer's Side*, 1891)

What are the complaints of the farmer?

Were they justified?

(The Grange movement gave way to a broader movement, known as Populism. While the issues of the farmer were still a priority, other grievances were addressed by the Populist movement.)

POPULIST PARTY PLATFORM

We declare, therefore—

First.—That the union of the labor forces of the United States this day consummated shall be permanent and perpetual; may its spirit enter into all hearts for the salvation of the Republic and the uplifting of mankind.

Second.—Wealth belongs to him who creates it, and every dollar taken from industry without an equivalent is robbery. "If any will not work, neither shall he eat." The interests of rural and civil labor are the same; their enemies are identical.

Third.—We believe that the time has come when the railroad corporations will either own the people or the people must own the railroads; and should the government enter upon the work of owning and managing all railroads, we should favor an amendment to the constitution by which all persons engaged in the government service shall be placed under a civil-service regulation of the most rigid character, so as to prevent the increase of the power of the national administration by the use of such additional government employees.

Finance.—We demand a national currency, safe, sound, and flexible issued by the general government only, a full legal tender for all debts, public and private, and that without the use of banking corporations; a just, equitable, and efficient means of distribution direct to the people, at a tax not to exceed 2 per center, per annum, to be provided as set forth in the sub-treasury plan of the Farmers' Alliance, or a better system; also by payments in discharge of its obligations for public improvements.

1. We demand free and unlimited coinage of silver and gold at the present legal ratio of 16 to 1.
2. We demand that the amount of circulating medium be speedily increased to not less than $50 per capita.
3. We demand a graduated income tax.
4. We believe that the money of the country should be kept as much as possible in the hands of the people, and hence we demand that all State and national revenues shall be limited to the necessary expenses of the government, economically and honestly administered.
5. We demand that postal savings banks be established by the government for the safe deposit of the earnings of the people and to facilitate exchange.

TRANSPORTATION.—Transportation being a means of exchange and a public necessity, the government should own and operate the railroads in the interest of the people. The telegraph and telephone, like the post-office system, being a necessity for the transmission of news, should be owned and operated by the government in the interest of the people.

LAND.—The land, including all the natural sources of wealth, is the heritage of the people, and should not be monopolized for speculative purposes, and alien ownership of land should be prohibited. All land now held by railroads and other corporations in excess of their actual needs, and all lands now owned by aliens should be reclaimed by the government and held for actual settlers only.

EXPRESSION OF SENTIMENTS

Your Committee on Platform and Resolutions beg leave unanimously to report the following.

Whereas, Other questions have been presented for our considerations, we hereby submit the following, not as a part of the Platform of the People's Party, but as resolutions expressive of the sentiment of this Convention.

1. RESOLVED, That we demand a free ballot and a fair count in all elections and pledge ourselves to secure it to every legal voter without Federal intervention, through the adoption by the States of the unperverted Australian or secret ballot system.

2. RESOLVED, That the revenue derived from a graduated income tax should be applied to the burden of taxation now levied upon the domestic industries of this country.

3. RESOLVED, That we pledge our support to fair and liberal pensions to ex-Union soldiers and sailors.

4. RESOLVED, That we condemn the fallacy of protecting American labor under   the present system, which opens our ports to the pauper and criminal classes of the world and crowds out our wage-earners; and we denounce the present ineffective laws against contract labor, and demand the further restriction of undesirable emigration.

5. RESOLVED, That we cordially sympathize with the efforts of organized workingmen to shorten the hours of labor, and demand a rigid enforcement of the existing eight-hour law on Government work, and ask that a penalty clause be added to the said law.

6. RESOLVED, That we regard the maintenance of large standing army of mercenaries, known as the Pinkerton system, as a menace to our liberties, and we demand its abolition; and we condemn the recent invasion of the Territory of   Wyoming by the hired assassins of plutocracy, assisted by Federal officers.

7. RESOLVED, That we commend to the favorable consideration of the people and the reform press the legislative system known as the initiative and referendum.

8. RESOLVED, That we favor a constitutional provision limiting the office of President and Vice-President to one term, and providing for the election of Senators of the United States by a direct vote of the people.

9. RESOLVED, That we oppose any subsidy or national aid to any private corporation for any purpose.

10. RESOLVED, That this convention sympathize with the Knights of Labor.

Examine the platform of the Populist Party. How many of their resolutions were eventually adopted?

(William Jennings Bryan became the spokesman for the Populist cause. He is best remembered for his Cross of Gold speech.)

BRYAN'S CROSS OF GOLD SPEECH

"You come to us and tell us that the great cities are in favor of the gold standard; we reply that the great cities rest upon our broad and fertile prairies. Burn down your cities and leave our farms, and your cities will spring up again as if by magic; but destroy our farms and the grass will grown in the streets of every city in the country....

Having behind us the producing masses of this nation and the world, supported by the commercial interests, the laboring interests, and the toilers everywhere, we will answer their demands for a gold standard by saying to them: You shall not press down upon the brow of labor this crown of thorns, you shall not crucify mankind upon a cross of gold."

Why did the Populists oppose the gold standard?

Who does Bryan say favors the gold standard?

(During the late 1800s, black Americans were engaged in debate over how blacks could best take advantage of educational opportunities. Booker T. Washington argued that blacks should assume a "non-antagonistic" role, while W.E.B. DuBois advanced a more aggressive role for blacks.)

TWO VIEWS ON BLACKS AND EDUCATION

Booker T. Washington

"To those of my race who depend on bettering their condition in a foreign land or who underestimate the importance of cultivating friendly relations with the southern white man, who is their next-door neighbor, I would say: Cast down your bucket where you are—cast it down in making friends in every manly way of the people of all races by whom we are surrounded.

Cast it down in agriculture, mechanics, in commerce, in domestic service, and in the professions. No race can prosper till it learns that here is as much dignity in tilling a field as in writing a poem."

W.E.B. DuBois

"Mr. Washington distinctly asks that black people give up, at least for the present, three things,—First, political power. Second, insistence on Civil Rights. Third, higher education of Negro youth,—and concentrate all their energies on industrial education...the accumulation of wealth, and the conciliation of the South...As a result of this tender of the palm branch, what has been the result? In these years there have occurred: (1) the disenfranchisement for the Negro. (2) the legal creation of a distinct status of civil inferiority for the Negro. (3) the steady withdrawal of aid...for the higher training of the Negro."
(From Speeches by Booker T. Washington and W.E.B. DuBois.)

How can you account for the different approaches Washington and DuBois had for black education?

(As labor problems intensified in the latter half of the 19th century, nativism was on the rise. Many Americans sought to cut off the flow of emigrants to America.)

NATIVIST VIEWS

California Senator Miller, 1882:

"If we continue to permit the introduction of this strange people, with their peculiar civilization, until they form a considerable part of our population, what is to be the effect upon the American people and Anglo-Saxon civilization?

During the late depression in business affairs which existed for three or four years in California, while thousands of white men and women were walking the streets, begging and pleading for an opportunity to give their honest labor for any wages, the great steamers...discharged at the wharves of San Francisco their accustomed cargoes of Chinese....

If they should be admitted to citizenship, then there would be a new element introduced into the governing power of this nation, which would be the most...irresponsible [and] ignorant...."

Author Henry Pratt Fairchild, Immigration, 1913:

"According to the established law of economics, there are two ways in which immigration may operate to lower wages. First, by increasing the supply of labor in the country, and thereby diminishing the amount of remuneration which the individual laborer can command. Second, by introducing a body of laborers whose customary wage in the countries they come from, and whose corresponding standard of living is much lower than the prevailing standard in the new country....

It appears that [these] forces...can have only one logical outcome—namely, the depression of the wage scale of the American workman. If immigration has not absolutely lowered the wages and the standard of living of the American workman, it certainly has kept them from rising to the level that they otherwise would have reached...."

Author Madison Grant, The Passing of the Great Race, 1916:

"At the time of the Revolutionary War the settlers in the thirteen colonies were overwhelmingly Nordic, a very large majority being Anglo-Saxon in the most limited meaning of that term....

The Civil War, however, put a severe, perhaps fatal check to the development and expansion of this splendid type....The prosperity that followed the war attracted hordes of newcomers who were welcomed by the native Americans to operate factories, build railroads, and fill up the waste spaces—'developing the country' it was called.

These new immigrants were no longer exclusively members of the Nordic race as were the earlier ones who came of their own impulse to improve their social conditions....

We Americans must realize that the altruistic ideals which have controlled our social development during the past century and the maudlin sentimentalism that has made America 'an asylum for the oppressed,' are sweeping the nation toward a racial abyss. If the Melting Pot is allowed to boil without control...the type of native American of colonial descent will become...extinct...."

Author Edward A. Ross, Immigrants in Politics, early 1900s:

"The Italian historian and sociologist Ferrero, after reviewing our immigration policy, concludes that the Americans, far from being 'practical,' are really the mystics of the modern world. He says: 'To confer citizenship each year upon great numbers of men born and educated in foreign countries—men who come with ideas and sympathies totally out of spirit with the diverse conditions in the new country; to grant them political rights they do not want, and of which they have never thought; to compel them to declare allegiance to a political constitution which they often do not understand; to try to transform subjects of old European monarchies into free citizens of young American republics over night—is not all this to do violence to common sense?'"

What reasons are given for opposing immigration to the United States?

What flaws (if any) can you see in this reasoning?

Study immigration charts covering the period 1865-1900. Did immigration decrease during this period?

Chapter Ten
Imperialism

"He has marked the American people as His chosen nation to finally lead in the redemption of the world."—Albert J. Beveridge

With the western frontier closed in 1890, the continental United States had taken form. Yet the restless energy of the American spirit still existed. By the end of the 19th century America began to expand its political and economic influence on a more global basis. The last decade of the 19th century would end with a war against Spain and a considerable expansion of American territory. Manifest Destiny now applied to the world at large.

Was America justified in assuming the role of an imperialist power? How were America's relations with the great European powers affected by this new role? Did the acquisition of new territory help or harm the United States? George Washington's farewell address had warned America of the problems associated with "foreign entanglements," but this advice was virtually ignored in the late 19th and early 20th centuries. The entry of the United States into World War I in 1917 would shatter any pretense of American isolationism from world problems.

(In 1897, Alfred Thayer Mahan, a naval officer, produced a book entitled, The Influence of Sea Power Upon History. *In the book Mahan argued that all great powers (most notably Great Britain) had become great powers because of their strong navies. The book had a major influence on the policies of the United States.)*

THE INFLUENCE OF SEA POWER

"To affirm the importance of distant markets and the relation to them of our own immense powers of production, implies logically the recognition of the link that joins the products and the markets—that is, the carrying trade.... We shall not follow far this line of thought before there will dawn the realization of America's unique position, facing the older worlds of the East and West....

The opening of a canal through the Central American isthmus...by modifying the direction of trade routes will induce a great increase of commercial activity and carrying trade throughout the Caribbean Sea....Every position in that sea will have enhanced commercial and military value, and the canal itself will have become a strategic center of the most vital importance....It will be a link between the two oceans; but the use, unless most carefully guarded by treaties, will belong wholly to the belligerent which controls the sea by its naval power. In case of war, the U.S. will...be impotent, as against any of the great maritime powers, to control the Central American canal. Militarily speaking, and having reference to European complications only, the piercing of the isthmus is nothing but a disaster to the U.S., in the present state of her military naval preparation....

The U.S. is woefully unready, not only in fact, but in purpose, to assert in the Caribbean and Central America, a weight of influence proportioned to the extent of her interest. We have not the navy and, what is worse, we are not willing to have the navy, that will weigh seriously in any disputes with those nations whose interests will conflict there with our own....Yet were our sea frontier as strong as it now is weak, passive self-defense, whether in trade or war, would be but a poor policy, so long as this world continues to be one of struggle....Our self-imposed isolation in the matter of markets, and the decline of our shipping interest in the last thirty years, have coincided singularly with an actual remoteness of this continent from the life of the rest of the world....

Whether they will or no, Americans must now begin to look outward. The growing production of the country demands it. An increasing volume of public sentiment demands it. The position of the U.S., between the two Old Worlds and the two great oceans, makes the same claim, which will soon be strengthened by the creation of the new link joining the Atlantic and Pacific. The tendency will be maintained and increased by the growth of the European colonies in the Pacific, by the advancing civilization of Japan, and by the rapid peopling of our Pacific states with men who have all the aggressive spirit of the advanced line of national progress...."

(From Mahan's *The Influence of Sea Power*, 1897.)

How did Mahan view American naval capacity in 1897?

Explain how this work would have influenced American Policy?

(Although the majority of Americans were supportive of American expansionism, there were dissenting views. Consider the various viewpoints expressed on expansionism.)

TWO POSITIVE VIEWS ON IMPERIALISM

Beveridge's Speech

God has not been preparing the English-speaking and Teutonic peoples for a thousand years for nothing but vain and idle self-admiration. No. He made us master organizers of the world to establish system where chaos reigned. He has given us the spirit of progress to overwhelm the forces of reaction throughout the earth. He has made us adept in government that we may administer government among savage and senile peoples. Were it not for such a force as this the world would relapse into barbarism and night. And of all our race He has marked the American people as His chosen nation to finally lead in the redemption of the world.

(From Albert J. Beveridge, Speech in the U.S. Senate, 1900.)

Adams's Speech

The West Indies drift toward us, the Republic of Mexico hardly longer has an independent life, and the city of Mexico is an American town. With the completion of the Panama Canal all Central America will become part of our system. We have expanded into Asia, we have attracted the fragments of the Spanish dominions, and reaching out into China we have checked the advance of Russia and Germany....We are penetrating into Europe, and Great Britain especially is gradually assuming the position of a dependency....The United States will outweigh any single empire, if not all empires combined. The whole world will pay her tribute. Commerce will flow to her from both east and west, and the order which has existed from the dawn of time will be reversed.

(From Books Adams, *The New Empire*, 1902)

The Anti-Imperialistic League (1899)

We demand the immediate cessation of the war against liberty, begun by Spain and continued by us. We urge that Congress be promptly convened to announce to the Filipinos our purpose to concede to them the independence for which they have so long fought and which of right is theirs.

The United States have always protested against the doctrine of international law which permits the subjugation of the weak by the strong. A self-governing state cannot accept sovereignty over an unwilling people. The United States cannot act upon the ancient heresy that might makes right.

Imperialists assume that with the destruction of self-government in the Philippines by American hands, all opposition here will cease. This is a grievous error. Much as we abhor the war of "criminal aggression" in the Philippines, greatly as we regret that the blood of the Filipinos is on American hands, we more deeply resent the betrayal of American institutions at home. The real firing line is not in the suburbs of Manila. The foe is of our own household. The attempt of 1861 was to divide the country. That of 1899 is to destroy its fundamental principles and noblest ideals.

Whether the ruthless slaughter of the Filipinos shall end next month or next year is but an incident in a contest that must go on until the Declaration of Independence and the Constitution of the United States are rescued from the hands of the betrayers. Those who dispute about standards of value while the Republic is undermined will be listened to as little as those who would wrangle about the small economies of the household while the house is on fire. The training of a great people for a century, the aspiration for liberty of a vast immigration are forces that will hurl aside those who in the delirium of conquest seek to destroy the character of our institutions.

We deny that the obligation of all citizens to support their Government in times of grave National peril applies to the present situation. If an Administration may with impunity ignore the issues upon which it was chosen, deliberately create a condition of war anywhere on the face of the globe, debauch the civil service for spoils to promote the adventure, organize a truth-suppressing censorship and demand of all citizens, a suspension of judgement and their unanimous support while it chooses to continue the fighting, representative government itself is imperiled.

We propose to contribute to the defeat of any person or party that stands for the forcible subjugation of any people. We shall oppose for reelection all who in the White House or in Congress betray American liberty in pursuit of un-American gains. We still hope that both of our great political parties will support and defend the Declaration of Independence in the closing campaign of the century.

We hold, with Abraham Lincoln, that "no man is good enough to govern another man without that man's consent. When the white man governs himself, that is self-government, but when he governs himself and also governs another man, that is more than self-government—that is despotism." "Our reliance is in the love of liberty which God has planted in us. Our defense is in the spirit which prizes liberty as the heritage of all men in all lands. Those who deny freedom to others deserve it not for themselves, and under a just God cannot long retain it."

After considering the views on imperialism, make a statement for or against American imperialist policy of the 19th and 20th centuries.

(Theodore Roosevelt was in many ways ideally suited to be President of the United States during the imperialist age. His "New Nationalism" speech of 1910 is an example of his aggressive leadership.)

THEODORE ROOSEVELT'S NEW NATIONALISM

Theodore Roosevelt's "New Nationalism" speech (1910)

Our country—this great republic—means nothing unless it means the triumph of a real democracy, the triumph of popular government, and, in the long run, of an economic system under which each man shall be guaranteed the opportunity to show the best that there is in him....

I stand for the square deal. But when I say that I am for the square deal, I mean not merely that I stand for fair play under the present rules of the game, but that I stand for having those rules changed so as to work for a more substantial equality of opportunity and of reward for equally good service....

What is the "square deal" Theodore Roosevelt called for?

Chapter Eleven
America and the First World War

"The world must be made safe for democracy."—Woodrow Wilson

World War I began in Europe in 1914. The United States was not drawn into the global conflict until 1917. Despite Woodrow Wilson's 1916 campaign slogan *"he kept us out of war,"* America was unable to isolate itself from the problems of the old world. The war was a short one for the United States. American troops were not fully mobilized until the end of 1917, and by November, 1918 the war was over. Woodrow Wilson and the American delegation were destined to play a significant role at the peace talks in Paris beginning in 1919.

America's entry into World War I represents a turning point in American history. By entering the conflict in Europe and then taking the lead role at the Paris peace conference, the United States placed itself in the middle of European affairs. America would briefly retreat from this role in the 1930's during the Great Depression only to be brought back into world affairs on December 7, 1941, with the shattering events at Pearl Harbor.

WILSON'S NEW FREEDOM (1913)

We have itemized with some degree of particularity the things that ought to be altered and here are some of the chief items: A tariff which cuts us off from our proper part in the commerce of the world, violates the just principles of taxation, and makes the Government a facile instrument in the hands of private interests; a banking and currency system based upon the necessity of the government to sell its bonds fifty years ago and perfectly adapted to concentrating cash and restricting credits; an industrial system which, take it on all sides, financial as well as administrative, holds capital in leading strings, restricts the liberties and limits the opportunities of labor, and exploits without renewing or conserving the natural resources of the country; a body of agricultural activities never yet given the efficiency of great business undertakings or served as it should be through the instrumentality of science taken directly to the farm, or afforded the facilities of credit best suited to its practical needs; water courses undeveloped, waste places unreclaimed, forests untended, fast disappearing without plan or prospect of renewal, unregarded waste heaps at every mine.

(From Woodrow Wilson, First Inaugural Address, 1913.)

Outline the major planks of Wilson's domestic program.

WILSON ON AMERICAN IDEALS (1914)

My dream is that, as the years go on and the world knows more and more of America, it will also drink at these fountains of youth and renewal; that it also will turn to America for those moral inspirations which lie at the basis of all freedom; that the world will never fear America, unless it feels that it is engaged in some enterprise which is inconsistent with the rights of humanity; and that America will come into the full light of day when all shall know that she puts human rights above all other rights and that her flag is the flag not only of America, but of humanity.

(Germany's resumption of unrestricted submarine warfare in 1917 brought the United States to the brink of war. On March 1, 1917, American newspapers reported that the British had decoded a German dispatch to Mexico outlining plans to resume submarine warfare. The decoded message also contained evidence that Germany was asking Mexico to align itself against the United States. The so-called Zimmermann Note *was instrumental in leading America into war with Germany.)*

THE ZIMMERMANN TELEGRAM

"We intend to begin unrestricted submarine warfare on the first of February. We shall endeavor in spite of this to keep the United States neutral. In the event of this not succeeding, we make Mexico a proposal of alliance on the following basis: Make war together, make peace together, generous financial support, and an understanding on our part that Mexico is to reconquer the lost territory in Texas, New Mexico, and Arizona. The settlement in detail is left to you.

You will inform the president [of Mexico] of the above most secretly as soon as the outbreak of war with the United States is certain and add the suggestion that he should, on his own initiative, invite Japan to immediate adherence and at the same time mediate between Japan and ourselves.

Please call the president's attention to the fact that the unrestricted employment of our submarines now offers the prospect of compelling England to make peace within a few months. Acknowledge receipt."

What aspect of this telegram would have most angered Americans?

(Woodrow Wilson had campaigned in 1916 with the slogan, "He kept us out of war," but by April 2, 1917, he was forced to ask Congress for a declaration of war. The majority of Americans supported Wilson's position; however, there were voices of dissent. These voices were soon drowned out by the shouts of patriotism.)

WILSON'S WAR MESSAGE (APRIL 2, 1917)

"Our object now, as then, is to vindicate the principles of peace and justice in the life of the world as against selfish and autocratic power and to set up amongst the really free and self-governed peoples of the world such a concert of purpose and of action as will henceforth insure the observance of those principles.... The world must be made safe for democracy. Its peace must be planted upon the tested foundations of political liberty. We have no selfish ends to serve. We desire no conquest, no dominion. We seek no indemnities for ourselves, no material compensation for the sacrifices we shall freely make. We are but one of the champions of the rights of mankind. We shall be satisfied when those rights have been made as secure as the faith and freedom of nations can make them."

What role does Wilson see for America in the war?

What is our purpose for entering the war?

SENATOR NORRIS'S WARNING

"We are taking a step today that is fraught with untold danger. We are going into war upon the command of gold. We are going to run the risk of sacrificing millions of our countrymen's lives in order that other countrymen may coin their lifeblood into money.... We are about to do the bidding of wealth's terrible mandate. By our act we will make millions of our countrymen suffer, and the consequences of it may well be that millions of our brethren must shed their life blood, millions of broken-hearted women must weep, millions of children must suffer the cold, and millions of babes must die from hunger, and all because we want to preserve the commercial right of American citizens to deliver munitions of war to belligerent nations."

Why did Senator Norris oppose the entry of the U.S. into the war?

(When the war ended, in November, 1918, America was looked to for guidance in formulating a peace treaty. Woodrow Wilson headed the American delegation to Paris in 1919. The most controversial aspect of the Versailles Treaty of 1919 was the League of Nations. American opinion of the league was, at best, "indecisive.")

WILSON SUPPORTS THE LEAGUE

America is going to grow more and more powerful; and the more powerful she is the more inevitable it is that she should be trustee for the peace of the world.... All Europe knew that we were doing an American thing when we put the Covenant of the League of Nations at the beginning of the treaty.... The most cynical men I had to deal with...before our conferences were over...all admitted that the League of Nations, which they had deemed an ideal dream, was a demonstrable, practical necessity. This treaty cannot be carried out without the League of Nations....

The rest of the world is necessary to us; if you want to put it on that basis. I do not like to put it on that basis. That is not the American basis. America does not want to feed upon the rest of the world. She wants to feed it and serve it. America...is the only national idealistic force in the world, and idealism is going to save the world.... That is the program of civilization.

(From Woodrow Wilson, Speech at Helena, Montana, November 1919.)

LODGE WARNS AGAINST THE LEAGUE

Never forget that this league is primarily—I might say overwhelmingly—a political organization, and I object strongly to having the politics of the United States turn upon disputes where deep feeling is aroused but in which we have no direct interest. It will tend to delay the Americanization of our great population, and it is more important not only to the United States but to the peace of the world to make all these people good Americans than it is to determine that some piece of territory should belong to one European country rather than to another. For this reason I wish to limit strictly our interference in the affairs of Europe and of Africa. We have interests of our own account, but the less we undertake to play the part of umpire and thrust ourselves into European conflicts the better for the United States and for the world.

(Henry Cabot Lodge, Speech in the Senate, August 1919.)

Which of the two views on the League of Nations most clearly represented American opinion in 1919?

(The Russian Revolution of November 1917 created a new fear in America: the fear of communism. Wilson's Attorney General, Mitchell Palmer, was intent on checking the "Reds.")

PALMER SPEAKS AGAINST THE REDS

Behind, and underneath, my own determination to drive from our midst the agents of Bolshevism...I have discovered the hysterical methods of these revolutionary humans.... People...ask questions which involve the reasons for my acts against the "Reds." I have been asked...to what extent deportation will check radicalism in this country. Why not ask what will become of the United States Government if these alien radicals...carry out the principles of the Communist Party?....

In place of the United States Government we should have the horror and terrorism of Bolshevik tyranny such as is destroying Russia now.... The whole purpose of communism appears to be a mass formation of the criminals of the world to overthrow the decencies of private life, to usurp property...to disrupt the present order of life regardless of health, sex or religious rights....

These are the revolutionary tenets of...the Communist Internationale.... These include the I.W.W.'s, the most radical socialists, misguided anarchists, the agitators who oppose the limitations of unionism, the moral perverts and the hysterical neurasthenic women who abound in communism.

(From A. Mitchell Palmer, The Case Against the Reds, The Forum, February 1920.)

According to Mitchell Palmer, why were the Reds dangerous?

Chapter Twelve
Prosperity and Depression

"I am prepared under my constitutional duty to recommend the measures that a stricken nation in the midst of a stricken world may require."—Franklin Delano Roosevelt

At the conclusion of the First World War America was ready to retreat from world affairs and concentrate on the business of America. Warren G. Harding took the presidential oath of office in 1921 and began to preside over an unprecedented business boom. His successor Calvin Coolidge declared that *"the business of America is business."* The boom would not last. By 1929 the stock market crash, combined with a general downturn in the international economy, stalled the business of America and sent the world into the Great Depression.

The election of Franklin D. Roosevelt in 1932 was a watershed event in American history. Roosevelt introduced dramatic changes to the American political and economic system. The New Deal, as Roosevelt called his program of reform, would entail wholesale government intervention into the American economy. Many of these reforms are still present and continue to impact the American economy.

(The modern Ku Klux Klan got its start in the 1920's. More vocal and violent than the earlier Klan, the new Klan saw its power base grow beyond the Old South. American author, H.L. Mencken, in his typical style, offers us a cynical view of the Klan.)

MENCKEN ON THE KU KLUX KLAN

The remoter and more forlorn yokels have risen against their betters—and...their uprising is as hopeless as it is idiotic.... The truth is that the strength of the Klan, like the strength of the Anti-Saloon League...has always been greatly overestimated. Even in the most barbarous reaches of the South...it met with vigorous challenge from the start, and there are not three Confederate States to-day in which, on a fair plebiscite, it could hope to prevail. The fact that huge hordes of Southern politicians jumped into night-shirts when it began is not proof that it was actually mighty; it is only proof that politicians are cowards and idiots. Of late all of them have been seeking to rid themselves of the tell-tale tar and feathers; they try to ride the very genuine wave of aversion and disgust as they tried to ride the illusory wave of popularity. As the Klan falls everywhere, the Anti-Saloon League tends to fall with it.

(From H.L. Mencken, *Prejudices: Sixth Series*, 1927.)

How accurate was Mencken in his assessment of the Klan?

(The 18th amendment to the Constitution was ratified in 1919 thus making the sale or consumption of "intoxicating liquors" illegal. The law of the land was ignored by many, but alcoholic consumption was reduced by the 18th amendment.

Public opinion of the merits of prohibition varied greatly. In 1924, the famous trial lawyer, Clarence Darrow, and John Haynes, a noted prohibitionist, offered their opinions on the 18th amendment.)

CLARENCE DARROW ATTACKS PROHIBITION

I have been raised, we'll assume, to drink beer. Nature ferments the cider and the grape juice, and the world has always used it—the good and the bad alike—in churches also. They have used it on all occasions. They have used it for the festivity of the wedding and the sorrow of the burial, for all time. And probably three fourths of the people of the earth believe they should have a perfect right to use it—and at least 40 percent of the people of the United States.

If the doctrine should prevail that when 60 percent of the people of a country believe that certain conduct should be a criminal offense and for that conduct they must send the 40 percent to jail, then liberty is dead and freedom is gone. They will first destroy the 40 percent, and then turn and destroy each other.

(From a 1924 speech by Clarence Darrow)

JOHN HAYNES SUPPORTS PROHIBITION

To that definition of the Prohibition Amendment I say briefly, to the point—"Tommyrot." The Eighteenth Amendment to the Constitution is not sumptuary legislation. It has nothing to do with sumptuary legislation. From beginning to end, it is social legislation.

You say, "Why has the state any right to dictate to me what I shall drink?" The state hasn't any right to dictate to you what you shall drink, provided that what you drink affects yourself alone and does not affect society at large. If any man should say to me or prove to me upon the basis of social experience and laboratory experiments that the drinking of a cup of coffee does to society what the drinking of a glass of whiskey does, then I should say that legislation against coffee, like legislation against whiskey, was justified—justified by its social effects, justified by the fact that the safety and happiness of us all must be protected from the invasion of the one or the two.

(From John Haynes public debate, 1924.)

Do the arguments against alcohol today bear any resemblance to the prohibition controversy of the 1920's?

(While the Senate failed to ratify the Versailles Treaty, it did not signal the beginning of American isolationism. Indeed, America was deeply involved in world affairs in the 1920's. The Kellogg/Briand Pact, ratified in 1928, was an attempt to outlaw war.)

THE KELLOGG PEACE PACT (1928)

The President of the German Reich, the President of the United States of America, His Majesty the King of the Belgians, the President of the French Republic, His Majesty the King of Great Britain, Ireland and the British Dominions beyond the Seas, Emperor of India, His Majesty the King of Italy, His Majesty the Emperor of Japan, the President of the Republic of Poland, the President of the Czechoslovak Republic,

Deeply sensible of their solemn duty to promote the welfare of mankind; persuaded that the time has come when a frank renunciation of war as an instrument of national policy should be made to the end that the peaceful and friendly relations now existing between their peoples may be perpetuated;

Convinced that all changes in their relations with one another should be sought only by pacific means and be the result of a peaceful and orderly process, and that any signatory power which shall hereafter seek to promote its national interests by resort to war should be denied the benefits furnished by this treaty;

Hopeful that, encouraged by their example, all the other nations of the world will join in this humane endeavor and by adhering to the present treaty as soon as it comes into force bring their peoples within the scope of its beneficent provisions, thus uniting the civilized nations of the world in a common renunciation of war as an instrument of their national policy;

Have decided to conclude a treaty and for that purpose have appointed as their respective plenipotentiaries:...

Who, having communicated to one another their full powers found in good and due form have agreed upon the following articles:

149

ART. 1. The high contracting parties solemnly declare in the names of their respective peoples that they condemn recourse to war for the solution of international controversies, and renounce it as an instrument of national policy in their relations with one another.

ART. 2. The high contracting parties agree that the settlement or solution of all disputes or conflicts of whatever nature or of whatever origin they may be, which may arise among them, shall never be sought except by pacific means.

ART. 3. The present treaty shall be ratified by the high contracting parties named in the preamble in accordance with their respective constitutional requirements, and shall take effect as between them as soon as all their several instruments of ratification shall have been deposited at Washington.

This treaty shall, when it has come into effect as prescribed in the preceding paragraph, remain open as long as may be necessary for adherence by all the other powers of the world. Every instrument evidencing the adherence of a power shall be deposited at Washington and the treaty shall immediately upon such deposit become effective as between the power thus adhering and the other powers parties hereto....

What measures did the Kellogg Pact advocate in order to prevent wars?

(When the Great Depression hit in 1929, Herbert Hoover insisted that "prosperity is just around the corner." He believed that individuals, by pulling together, could beat the depression. His philosophy was basically the same as most Americans in 1929. His views were clearly stated in 1928, a full year before the crash of 29".

HOOVER ON RUGGED INDIVIDUALISM

During 150 years we have builded up a form of self-government and a social system which is peculiarly our own...It is the American system...it is founded upon the conception that only through ordered liberty, freedom and equal opportunity to the individual will his initiative and enterprise spur on the march of progress...

During the war we necessarily turned to the Government to solve every difficult economic problem...To a large degree we regimented our whole people temporarily into a socialistic state. However justified in time of war, if continued in peace time it would destroy not only our American system but with it our progress and freedom as well.

When the war closed,...We were challenged with a peacetime choice between the American system of rugged individualism and a European philosophy of diametrically opposed doctrines—doctrines of paternalism and state socialism. The acceptance of these ideas would have meant the destruction of self-government through centralization of government. It would have meant the undermining of the individual initiative and enterprise though which our people have grown to unparalleled greatness.

The Republican Party...restored the Government to its position as an umpire instead of a player in the economic game. For these reasons the American people have gone forward in progress while the rest of the world has halted, and some countries have even gone backwards...

There has been revived in this campaign, however, a series of proposals which, if adopted, would be a long step toward...the destructive operation of governmental conduct of commercial business. Because the country is faced with difficulty and doubt over certain national problems—that is, prohibition, farm relief and electrical power—our opponents propose that we must thrust government a long way into the business which give rise to these problems...

It is a false liberalism that interprets itself into the Government operation of commercial business. Every step of bureaucratizing of the business of our country poisons the very roots of liberalism—that is, political equality, free speech, free assembly, free press, and equality of opportunity. It is the road not to more liberty, but to less liberty...

(From a 1928 Hoover speech)

Why did Hoover resist government intervention into the American economy?

(By 1932 Hoover and F.D.R. were taking different views on how to handle the depression.)

HOOVER ON RELIEF

The proposals of our opponents will endanger or destroy our system.... I especially emphasize that promise to promote "employment for all surplus labor at all times." At first I could not believe that anyone would be so cruel as to hold out a hope so absolutely impossible of realization to these 10,000,000 who are unemployed. And I protest against such frivolous promises being held out to a suffering people. It is easy demonstrable that no such employment can be found. But the point I wish to make here and now is the mental attitude and spirit of the Democratic Party to attempt it. It is another mark of the character of the new deal and the destructive changes which mean the total abandonment of every principle upon which this government and the American system is founded. If it were possible to give this employment to 10,000,000 people by the Government, it would cost upwards of $9,000,000,000 a year.... It would pull down the employment of those who are still at work by the high taxes and the demoralization of credit upon which their employment is dependent.... It would mean the growth of a fearful bureaucracy which, once established, could never be dislodged.

(From Herbert Hoover, Campaign Address in New York, October, 1932)

FRANKLIN D. ROOSEVELT ON RELIEF

We have two problems: first, to meet the immediate distress; second, to build up on a basis of permanent employment.

As to "immediate relief," the first principle is that this nation, this national Government, if you like, owes a positive duty that no citizen shall be permitted to starve....

In addition to providing emergency relief, the Federal Government should and must provide temporary work wherever that is possible. You and I know that in the national forests, on flood prevention, and on the development of waterway projects that have already been authorized and planned but not yet executed, tens of thousands, and even hundreds of thousands of our unemployed citizens can be given at least temporary employment....

Third, the Federal Government should expedite the actual construction of public works already authorized....

Finally, in that larger field that looks ahead, we call for a coordinated system of employment exchanges, the advance planning of public works, and unemployment reserves.
(From Franklin D. Roosevelt, Campaign Address in Boston, October, 1932)

Why did most Americans react more favorably to Franklin D. Roosevelt's view in 1932?

(When Franklin D. Roosevelt became president, on March 4, 1933, he began almost immediately to attack the ravages of the Great Depression. In his first inaugural address, with his usual air of confidence, he spoke of the future of the United States.)

FRANKLIN D. ROOSEVELT'S FIRST INAUGURAL ADDRESS (1933)

"This is preeminently the time to speak the truth, the whole truth, frankly and boldly.... This great nation will endure as it has endured, will revive and will prosper. So, first of all, let me assert my firm belief that the only thing we have to fear is fear itself—nameless, unreasoning, unjustified terror which paralyzes needed efforts to convert retreat into advance.

Values have shrunken to fantastic levels; taxes have risen; our ability to pay has fallen;...the means of exchange are frozen;...farmers find no markets for their produce; the savings of many years...are gone.

More important, a host of unemployed citizens face the grim problem of existence, and an equally great number toil with little return.

Our greatest primary task is to put people to work.... It can be accomplished in part by direct recruiting by the government itself, treating the task as we would treat the emergency of war.

Hand in hand with this we must frankly recognize the overbalance of population in our industrial centers and...endeavor to provide a better use of the land for those best fitted for the land.

Finally...there must be a strict supervision of all banking and credits and investments; there must be an end to speculation with other people's money, and there must be provision for an adequate but sound currency.

I favor as a practical policy the putting of first things first. I shall spare no effort to restore world trade...but the emergency at home cannot wait on that accomplishment.

I am prepared under my constitutional duty to recommend

the measures that a stricken nation in the midst of a stricken world may require.

We do not distrust the future.... The people of the United States have not failed. In their need they have registered a mandate that they want direct, vigorous action.... They have made me the present instrument of their wishes. In the spirit of the gift I take it...."

How would you have reacted to this speech in 1933?

To what extent did Roosevelt carry through with his statements in this 1933 address?

(While Franklin D. Roosevelt planned and carried forth a massive assault on the Great Depression, it was not quite enough for everyone. The Socialist Party platform of 1932 called for even more government involvement in the American economy.)

THE SOCIALIST PARTY PLATFORM OF 1932

1. $5 billion for immediate relief.
2. A federal appropriation of $5 billion for public works and roads, reforestation, slum clearance, and decent homes for the workers, by federal government, states, and cities.
3. Legislation providing for the acquisition of land, buildings, and equipment necessary to put the unemployed to work producing food, fuel, and clothing, for the erection of houses for their own use.
4. The six-hour day and the five-day week without a reduction of wages.
5. A comprehensive and efficient system of free public employment agencies.
6. A compulsory system of unemployment compensation with adequate benefits, based on contributions by the government and by employers.
7. Old-age pensions for men and women sixty years of age and over.
8. Health and maternity insurance.
9. Improved system of workmen's compensation and accident insurance.
10. The abolition of child labor.
11. Government aid to farmers and small homeowners to protect them against mortgage foreclosures and a moratorium on sales for nonpayment of taxes by destitute farmers and unemployed workers.
12. Adequate minimum wage laws.

Social Ownership

1. Public ownership and democratic control of mines, forests, oil, and power resources; public utilities dealing with light and power, transportation and communication, and of all other basic industries...

Taxation

1. Steeply increased inheritance taxes and income taxes on the higher incomes and estates of both corporations and individuals....

Agriculture

Many of the foregoing measures for socializing the power, banking, and other industries, for raising living standards among the city workers, etc., would greatly benefit the farming population.

As special measures for agricultural upbuilding, we propose:

1. The reduction of tax burdens by a shift from taxes on farm property to taxes on incomes, inheritances, excess profits, and other similar forms of taxation.
2. Increased federal and state subsidies to road building and education and social services for rural communities.
3. The recreation of a federal marketing agency for the purchase and marketing of agricultural products.
4. The acquisition by bona fide cooperative societies and by governmental agencies of grain elevators, stockyards, packing houses, and warehouses, and the conduct of these services on a nonprofit basis. The encouragement of farmers' cooperative societies and of consumers' cooperatives in the cities, with a view of eliminating the middle-man.
5. The socialization of federal land banks and the extension by these banks of long-term credit to farmers at low rates of interest.
6. Social insurance against losses due to adverse weather conditions.

7. The creation of national, regional, and state land utilization boards for the purpose of discovering the best uses of the farming land of the country, in view of the joint needs of agriculture, industry, recreation, water supply, reforestation, etc., and to prepare the way for agricultural planning on a national and, ultimately, on a world scale....

Committed to this constructive program, the Socialist Party calls upon the nation's workers and upon all fair-minded and progressive citizens to unite with it in a might movement against the present drift into social disaster and in behalf of sanity, justice, peace, and freedom.

Examine the Socialist Party Platform carefully. How many of their proposals have been accepted over the years?

(One of the far left's most animated spokesmen was Huey P. Long, of Louisiana. Consider his 1933 "Share the Wealth" program.)

HUEY LONG'S SHARE THE WEALTH PROGRAM (1933)

What I have proposed is....

1. A capital levy tax on the property owned by any one person of 1% of all over $1,000,000; 2% of all over $2,000,000 etc., until, when it reaches fortunes of over $100,000,000, the government takes all above that figure; which means a limit on the size of any one man's fortune to something like $50,000,000—the balance to go to the government to spread out in its work among all the people.
2. An inheritance tax which does not allow any one person to receive more than $5,000,000 in a lifetime without working for it....
3. An income tax which does not allow any one person to receive more than $1,000,000 in one year, exclusive of taxes....

The foregoing program means all taxes paid by fortune holders at the top and none by the people at the bottom; the spreading of wealth among all the people and the breaking up of a system of Lords and Slaves in our economic life....

Then...the food of the land will feed, the raiment clothe, and the houses shelter all the people....

Then...EVERY MAN A KING.

(From Huey P. Long, *Every Man a King*, 1933.

How realistic was Mr. Long's program?

(in 1937 the Supreme Court placed severe restrictions on the New Deal. The "limiting view" of congressional power rendered by the Court caused Franklin Roosevelt, and his "brain trust," to rethink their approach to the depression.)

A LIMITING VIEW OF CONGRESSIONAL POWER

In determining how far the federal government may go in controlling intrastate transactions upon the ground that they "affect" interstate commerce, there is a necessary and well-established distinction between direct and indirect effects. The precise line can be drawn only as individual cases arise, but the distinction is clear in principle....

If the commerce clause were construed to reach all enterprises and transactions which could be said to have an indirect effect upon interest rate commerce, the federal authority would embrace practically all the activities of the people and the authority of the state over its domestic concerns would exist only by suffrance of the federal government....

There would be virtually no limit to the federal power, and for all practical purposes we should have a completely centralized government. We must consider the provisions here in light of this distinction.

The question of chief importance relates to the provisions of the code as to the hours and wages of those employed....It is plain that these requirements are imposed in order to govern the details of defendants' management of their local business. The persons employed...are not employed in interstate commerce. Their wages have no direct relation to interstate commerce....

The authority of the federal government may not be pushed to such an extreme.

(From the Majority Opinion of the United States Supreme Court by Mr. Chief Justice Charles E. Hughes, Schechter v. United States, 295 U.S. 495, 1935.)

What restrictions did the Court place on New Deal legislation?

How did Franklin Roosevelt attempt to counter this decision by the Supreme Court?

(Organized labor was given a big boost by the New Deal. The National Labor Relations Act, of July, 1935, basically gave labor a free rein to organize and to collectively bargain. This Act was among the most important pieces of legislation in labor history.)

THE NATIONAL LABOR RELATIONS ACT (1935)

Section I

The inequality of bargaining power between employees who do not possess full freedom of association or actual liberty of contract, and employers who are organized in the corporate or other forms of ownership association...tend to aggravate recurrent business depressions by depressing wage rates and the purchasing power of wage earners in industry and by preventing the stabilization of competitive wage rates and working conditions within and between industries.

Section VII

Employees shall have the right of self-organization, to form, join, or assist labor organizations, to bargain collectively through representatives of their own choosing, and to engage in concerted activities, for the purpose of collective bargaining or other mutual aid or protection.

Section VIII

It shall be an unfair labor practice for an employer —

(1) To interfere with, restrain, or coerce employees in the exercise of their rights guaranteed in section 7.

(2) To dominate or interfere with the formation or administration of any labor organization or contribute financial or other support to it...

(5) To refuse to bargain collectively with the representatives of his employees...

(U.S. Statutes at Large, XLIX (1935))

163

Why did labor leaders view this act as the "Magna Carta" of labor legislation?

Chapter Thirteen
World War II

"When an epidemic of physical disease starts to spread, the community approves and joins in a quarantine of the patients in order to protect the health of community against the spread of the disease."—Franklin Delano Roosevelt

World War II began in Europe in 1939. America maintained her neutrality until December 7, 1941, Pearl Harbor Day. The attack on Pearl Harbor brought America into a war that was very different from World War I. Instead of a brief fight, America found itself in a four year struggle. Over 500,000 Americans lost their lives in this war. Additionally, the war brought about the development of the Atomic Bomb, which would change the face of war for all time.

World War II secured the United States as the world's greatest superpower. America's role as a global leader has grown steadily since the end of World War II in 1945. Many maintain that the United States has overextended itself, and should resume a more detached role in global politics. The prospect of the United States retreating from its global leadership position seems unlikely from the vantage point of the 21st century.

(When the Japanese invaded Manchuria in 1931, the first steps toward World War II had begun. Secretary of State Henry Stimson addressed the situation in 1931.)

THE STINSON DOCTRINE

The last remaining administrative authority of the Government of the Chinese Republic in South Manchuria, as it existed prior to September 18, 1931, has been destroyed.... In view of the present situation and of its own rights and obligations therein, the American Government deems it to be its duty to notify both the Imperial Japanese Government and the Government of the Chinese Republic that it cannot admit the legality of any situation de facto nor does it intend to recognize any treaty or agreement entered into between those Governments...which may impair the treaty rights of the United States or its citizens in China, including those which relate to the sovereignty, the independence, or the territorial and administrative integrity of the Republic of China, nor to the international policy relative to China, commonly known as the open door policy; and that it does not intend to recognize any situation, treaty, or agreement which may be brought about by means contrary to the covenants and obligations of the Pact of Paris of...1928.

(From *Foreign Relations of the United States: Japan* 1931-1941. I, 1943)

What was the American position in regards to the Japanese invasion of Manchuria?

(As Hitler began his aggressive actions in Europe, and Japan persisted in its occupation of China, many Americans began to debate the role America should take in these affairs.)

GERALD P. NYE: THE ISOLATIONIST VIEWPOINT

There can be no objection to any hand our Government may take which strives to bring peace to the world so long as that hand does not tie 130,000,000 people into another world death march.

I very much fear that we are once again being caused to feel that the call is upon America to police a world that chooses to follow insane leaders. Once again we are baited to thrill to a call to save the world.

We reach now a condition on all fours with that prevailing just before our plunge into the European war in 1917. Will we blindly repeat that futile venture? Can we easily forget that we won nothing we fought for then—that we lost every cause declared to be responsible for our entry then?

(From Senator Gerald P. Nye, Statement in the New York Times, October, 1937)

FRANKLIN D. ROOSEVELT AND THE CONTAGION OF WAR

It seems to be unfortunately true that the epidemic of world lawlessness is spreading.

When an epidemic of physical disease starts to spread, the community approves and joins in a quarantine of the patients in order to protect the health of the community against the spread of the disease....

War is a contagion, whether it be declared or undeclared. It can engulf states and peoples remote from the original scene of hostilities. We are determined to keep out of war, yet we cannot insure ourselves against the disastrous effects of war and the dangers of involvement. We are adopting such measures as will minimize our risk of involvement, but we cannot have complete protection in a world of disorder in which confidence and security have broken down....

Most important of all, the will for peace on the part of peace-loving nations must express itself to the end that nations that may be tempted to violate their agreements and the rights of others will desist from such a course. There must be positive endeavors to preserve peace.

(From Franklin D. Roosevelt, Speech at Chicago, October, 1937)

Why did Senator Nye oppose American involvement?

What is Franklin D. Roosevelt saying about world events?

(In January, 1941, ten months before Pearl Harbor, Franklin D.

Roosevelt delivered his famous Four Freedoms speech.)

FRANKLIN D. ROOSEVELT'S "FOUR FREEDOMS" SPEECH (1941)

In the future days, which we seek to make secure, we look forward to a world founded upon four essential human freedoms.

The first is freedom of speech and expression—everywhere in the world.

The second is freedom of every person to worship God in his own way—everywhere in the world.

The third is freedom from want—which, translated into world terms, means economic understandings which will secure to every nation a healthy peacetime life for its inhabitants—everywhere in the world.

The fourth is freedom from fear—which, translated into world terms, means a worldwide reduction of armaments to such a point and in such a thorough fashion that no nation will be in a position to commit an act of physical aggression against any neighbor—anywhere in the world....

What were the four freedoms discussed by Roosevelt? How might this speech have been received by the European powers in 1941?

(Franklin D. Roosevelt agreed in 1941 to begin a lend-lease

arrangement with Great Britain. Basically, this agreement provided a way for the United States to supply arms to Great Britain. Many argued that this was a violation of American neutrality.)

AN ANTI-LAND-LEASE VIEW

We confront a terrible emergency; yes. But the worst of the emergency, in my view, is the insinuating proposal that to keep others free, we must become less free ourselves.... This so-called lending-leasing bill not only invites us closer to the grim event of war itself...but it lends essential congressional prerogatives to the President and leases a new portion of the Constitution to the White House—and all unnecessary in order to aid England short of war....

This bill hands the President...all these vital American resources...plus the authority to purchase or manufacture or "otherwise procure" war supplies, as he sees fit, either at home or abroad.... He can lease these resources or lend them or give them away on whatever terms may suit his fancy. He is almoner and armorer to the world....

This is a license to arm half or more of the earth out of our arsenals at a moment of grave danger, when we have not yet been able adequately even to arm ourselves.... I reject and deny the novel doctrine...that our American defense is thus at the mercy of any such far-flung manipulation of power politics in the Old World.

(From Senator Arthur H. Vandenberg, Speech in the United States Senate, February, 1941)

A PRO-LEND-LEASE VIEW

These are the provisions which it is said set up a dictatorship in the United States. But, may I ask what other officer of the Government of the United States than the President could or should be empowered to do these things? Congress cannot execute its own laws. That must be done by the Executive established by the Constitution.... The President...is also the Commander-in-Chief of the Army and Navy of the United States. Congress cannot divest him of this official character by statute. There is no other appropriate person or officer than the President who can carry out the will of Congress....

It has been suggested that the bill itself ought to name the countries which are to receive the aid which it provides. If the situation now existing were permanent, and not subject to daily or weekly changes, such a provision might be safe. But the situation is not permanent. We have seen one after another of the small nations of Europe overrun. At present England...Greece...and China...are the defenders of their right to exist. Tomorrow it may be some other nation.

(From Senator Alben W. Barkley, Speech in the United States Senate, February 1941)

Was Franklin Roosevelt justified in creating the lend-lease arrangement?

(The surprise attack on Pearl Harbor, December 7, 1941, made many Americans question how the United States could have been so unprepared. The Senate created a special investigative task force to study the circumstances surrounding the attack.)

MAJORITY REPORT OF JOINT COMMITTEE ON PEARL HARBOR ATTACK

The majority report (6 Democrats and 2 Republicans) of the Joint Committee on the Investigation of the Pearl Harbor Attack, July 20, 1946.

1. The December 7, 1941, attack on Pearl Harbor was an unprovoked act of aggression by the Empire of Japan. The treacherous attack was planned and launched while Japanese ambassadors, instructed with characteristic duplicity, were carrying on the pretense of negotiations with the Government of the United States, with a view to an amicable settlement of differences in the Pacific.
3. The diplomatic policies and actions of the United States provided no justifiable provocation whatever for the attack by Japan on this Nation...
4. The committee has found no evidence to support the charges, made before and during the hearing, that the President, the Secretary of State, the Secretary of War, or the Secretary of the Navy tricked, provoked, incited, cajoled, or coerced Japan into attacking this Nation in order that a declaration of war might be more easily obtained from the Congress. On the contrary, all evidence conclusively points to the fact that they discharged their responsibilities with distinction, ability, and foresight and in keeping with the highest traditions of our fundamental foreign policy.
5. The President, the Secretary of State, and high Government officials made every possible effort, without sacrificing our national honor and endangering our security, to avert war with Japan.

6. The disaster of Pearl Harbor was the failure...of the Army and the Navy to institute measures designed to detect an approaching hostile force, to effect a state of readiness commensurate with the realization that war was at hand, and to employ every facility at their command in repelling the Japanese.

9. The errors made by the Hawaiian commands were errors of judgment and not derelictions of duty.

11. The intelligence and War Plans Divisions of the War and Navy Departments failed:

(a) To give careful and thoughtful consideration to the intercepted messages from Tokyo to Honolulu...and to raise a question as to their significance...

(b) To be properly on the *qui vive* [alert] to receive the "one o'clock" intercept and to recognize in the message the fact that some Japanese military action would very possibly occur somewhere at 1 p.m., December 7 ...

(*Investigation of the Pearl Harbor Attack.* Senate Document No. 244, 79th Congress, 2nd Session, 251.52)

What were the conclusions of the Senate investigation?

Who was blamed for the attack?

(In 1942 President Roosevelt was persuaded to issue an executive order providing for the relocation of people of Japanese ancestry. Many of those placed in detention were American citizens.)

THE INTERNMENT OF JAPANESE AMERICANS

"Whereas the successful prosecution of the war requires every possible protection against espionage and against sabotage to national-defense materials, national-defense premises, and national-defense utilities....

Now, therefore, by virtue of the authority vested in me as President of the United States, and Commander in Chief of the Army and Navy, I hereby authorize and direct the Secretary of War and the military commanders whom he may from time to time designate, whenever he or any designated commander deems such action necessary or desirable, to prescribe military areas in such places and of such extent as he or the appropriate military commander may determine, from which any or all persons may be excluded, and with respect to which, the right of any person to enter, remain in, or leave shall be subject to whatever restrictions the Secretary of War or the appropriate military commander may impose in his decision....

I hereby further authorize and direct all executive departments, independent establishments and other federal agencies, to assist the Secretary of War or the said military commanders in carrying out this Executive Order, including the furnishing of medical aid, hospitalization, food, clothing, transportation, use of land, shelter, and other supplies, equipment, utilities, facilities, and services...."

Did the United States have the right to intern American citizens of Japanese descent?

(One of the most controversial aspects of World War II was the decision to drop the atomic bomb on Japan. The ultimate decision was left to President Harry S Truman.)

A PLEA AGAINST USING THE BOMB

The development of nuclear power not only constitutes an important addition to the technological and military power of the United States, but creates grave political and economic problems for the future of this country.

Nuclear bombs cannot possibly remain a "secret weapon" at the exclusive disposal of this country for more than a few years. The scientific facts on which their construction is based are well known to scientists of other countries. Unless an effective international control of nuclear explosives is instituted, a race for nuclear armaments is certain to ensue following the first revelation of our possession of nuclear weapons to the world. Within ten years other countries may have nuclear bombs.... In the war to which such an armaments race is likely to lead, the United States, with its agglomeration of population and industry in comparatively few metropolitan districts, will be at a disadvantage over large areas.

We believe that these considerations make the use of nuclear bombs for an early unannounced attack against Japan inadvisable. If the United States were to be the first to release this new means of indiscriminate destruction upon mankind, we would sacrifice public support throughout the world, precipitate the race for armaments, and prejudice the possibility of reaching international agreement on the future control of such weapons.

(From the Committee on Social and Political Implication, Report to the Secretary of War, June 1945)

PRESIDENT TRUMAN'S VIEW

I realize the tragic significance of the atomic bomb.

Its production and its use were not lightly undertaken by this Government. But we knew that our enemies were on the search for it. We know now how close they were in finding it. And we know the disaster which would come to this nation, and to all peaceful nations, to all civilizations, if they had found it first.

That is why we felt compelled to undertake the long and uncertain and costly labor of discovery and production.

We won the race of discovery against the Germans.

Having found the bomb, we have used it. We have used it against those who attacked us without warning at Pearl Harbor, against those who have starved and beaten and executed American prisoners of war, against those who have abandoned the pretense of obeying the international laws of warfare. We have used it in order to shorten the agony of war, in order to save the lives of thousands and thousands of young Americans.

We shall continue to use it until we completely destroy Japan's power to make war. Only a Japanese surrender will stop us.

(From Harry S Truman, Radio Address, August 1945)

Chapter Fourteen
The Cold War

"I believe that it must be the policy of the United States to support free peoples who are resisting attempted subjugation by armed minorities or by outside pressures."—Harry S Truman

When Franklin Roosevelt, Winston Churchill, and Joseph Stalin met at Yalta in February of 1945, the war in Europe was not yet over and the war in the Pacific was still raging. The decisions made at Yalta helped set the stage for an ideological war between the United States and the Soviet Union, which lasted until the early 1990's. This war of ideologies became known as the Cold War. It must be noted that the Cold War at times became very hot. Over 100,000 American lives were lost during the Korean and Vietnam conflicts. Indeed, the war against communism proved to be very costly.

With the collapse of the Berlin Wall and the subsequent breakup of the Soviet Union the United States declared itself the victor of the Cold War. With the dawn of the 21st century historians are beginning to evaluate the Cold War in an entirely different manner than was possible before. Is the world a safer place than before the breakup of the Soviet Union? What restraints are being placed on the United States now that it is the lone superpower in the world?

(The Yalta Conference was perhaps the most important of all the wartime conferences. Roosevelt has been criticized for having been too conciliatory at Yalta.)

THE YALTA CONFERENCE

II. DECLARATION ON LIBERATED EUROPE

The following declaration has been approved:

The Premier of the Union of Soviet Socialist Republics, the Prime Minister of the United Kingdom and the President of the United States of America have consulted with each other in the common interests of the peoples of their countries and those of liberated Europe. They jointly declare their mutual agreement to concert during the temporary period of instability in liberated Europe the policies of their three Governments in assisting the peoples liberated from the domination of Nazi Germany and the peoples of the former Axis satellite states of Europe to solve by democratic means their pressing political and economic problems.

The establishment of order in Europe and the rebuilding of national economic life must be achieved by processes which will enable the liberated peoples to destroy the last vestiges of nazism and fascism and to create democratic institutions of their own choice. This is a principle of the Atlantic Charter—the right of all peoples to choose the form of government under which they will live—the restoration of sovereign rights and self-government to those people who have been forcibly deprived of them by the aggressor nations.

To foster the condition in which the liberated peoples may exercise these rights, the three Governments will jointly assist the people in any European liberated state or former Axis satellite state in Europe where, in their judgment conditions require, (a) to establish conditions of internal peace; (b) to carry out emergency measures for the relief of distressed peoples; (c) to form interim governmental authorities broadly representative of all democratic elements in the population and pledged to the earliest possible establishment through free elections of Governments responsive to the will of the people; and (d) to facilitate where necessary the holding of such elections.

The three Governments will consult the other United Nations and provisional authorities or other Governments in Europe when matters of direct interest to them are under consideration.

When, in the opinion of the three Governments, conditions in any European liberated state or any former Axis satellite state in Europe make such action necessary, they will immediately consult together on the measures necessary to discharge the joint responsibilities set forth in this declaration.

By this declaration we reaffirm our faith in the principles of the Atlantic Charter, our pledge in the Declaration by the United Nations and our determination to build in cooperation with other peace-loving nations world order, under law, dedicated to peace, security, freedom and general well-being of the European states.

VII. POLAND

The following declaration on Poland was agreed by the conference:

"A new situation has been created in Poland as a result of her complete liberation by the Red Army. This calls for the establishment of a Polish Provisional Government which can be more broadly based than was possible before the recent liberation of the western part of Poland.

The Provisional Government which is now functioning in Poland should therefore be reorganized on a broader democratic basis with the inclusion of democratic leaders from Poland itself and from Poles abroad. This new Government should then be called the Polish Provisional Government of National Unity.

What factors would have impacted Roosevelt's decisions at Yalta?

Were the agreements reached at Yalta fair?

(In March 1947 President Truman unveiled his Truman Doctrine. The doctrine pledged to support all nations seeking to resist subjugation.)

THE TRUMAN DOCTRINE

The United States has received from the Greek Government an urgent appeal for financial and economic assistance. Preliminary reports...corroborate the statement of the Greek Government that assistance is imperative if Greece is to survive as a free nation...

The very existence of the Greek state is today threatened by the terrorist activities of several thousand armed men, led by Communists, who defy the Government's authority...

Meanwhile, the Greek Government is unable to cope with the situation. The Greek army is small and poorly equipped. It needs supplies and equipment if it is to restore the authority to the Government throughout Greek territory...

Greece's neighbor, Turkey, also deserves our attention...The circumstances in which Turkey finds itself today are...different from those of Greece. Turkey has been spared the disasters that have beset Greece....Nevertheless, Turkey now needs our support.

Since the war Turkey has sought financial assistance from Great Britain and the United States for the purpose of effecting that modernization necessary for the maintenance of its national integrity.

That integrity is essential to the preservation of order in the Middle East....

I believe that it must be the policy of the United States to support free peoples who are resisting attempted subjugation by armed minorities or by outside pressures.

I believe that our help should be primarily through economic and financial aid, which is essential to economic stability and orderly political processes....

The seeds of totalitarian regimes are nurtured by misery and want. They spread and grow in the evil soil of poverty and strife. They reach their full growth when the hope of a people for a better life has died.

We must keep that hope alive.

The free peoples of the world look to us for support in maintaining their freedoms.

If we falter in our leadership, we may endanger the peace of the world—and we shall surely endanger the welfare of our own Nation.

(*Congressional Record*, 80th Congress, 1st Session, 1947)

(In a commencement address at Harvard University in 1947, Secretary of State George Marshall announced a plan by which the Truman Doctrine could be implemented. Basically, it was to be through the use of American dollars.)

MARSHALL PLAN (1947)

It is logical that the United States should do whatever it is able to do to assist in the return of normal economic health in the world, without which there can be no political stability and no assured peace.

Our policy is directed not against any country or doctrine but against hunger, poverty, desperation and chaos. Its purpose should be the revival of a working economy in the world so as to permit the emergence of political and social conditions in which free institutions can exist....

Any government that is willing to assist in the task of recovery will find full cooperation, I am sure, on the part of the United States government. Any government which maneuvers to block the recovery of other countries cannot expect help from us. Furthermore, governments, political parties, or groups which seek to perpetuate human misery in order to profit therefrom, politically or otherwise, will encounter the opposition of the United States....

What is the basic rationale of the Marshall Plan?

Why did some members of Congress balk at this Plan?

(In keeping with his pledge to support the independence of all nations, in 1946 President Truman signed a proclamation giving the Philippines full independence.)

PROCLAMATION OF PHILIPPINE INDEPENDENCE (1946)

Whereas it has been the repeated declaration of the...government of the United States of America that full independence would be granted the Philippines as soon as the people of the Philippines were prepared to assume this obligation; and

Whereas the people of the Philippines have clearly demonstrated their capacity for self-government;...

Now, therefore, I, Harry S Truman,...do hereby recognize the independence of the Philippines as a separate and self-governing nation....

What factors would have influenced the United States to grant independence to the Philippine nation?

(Joseph McCarthy, a senator from Wisconsin, staked his political career on fighting communism. Few were exempt from McCarthy's attacks. In 1951 he attacked George C. Marshall, a war hero, and an important official in the Truman administration.)

MCCARTHY ATTACKS MARSHALL

It is when we return to an examination of General Marshall's record since the spring of 1942 that we approach an explanation of the carefully planned retreat from victory. Let us again review the Marshall record, as I have disclosed it from the sources available and all of them friendly. This grim and solitary man it was who, early in World War II, determined to put his impress upon our global strategy, political and military.

It was Marshall who, amid the din for a "second front now" from every voice of Soviet inspiration, sought to compel the British to invade across the Channel in the fall of 1942 upon penalty of our quitting the war in Europe....

It was a Marshall-sponsored memorandum, advising appeasement of Russia in Europe and the enticement of Russia into the far-eastern war, circulated at Quebec, which foreshadowed our whole course at Tehran, at Yalta, and until now in the Far East.

It was Marshall who, at Tehran, made common cause with Stalin on the strategy of the war in Europe and marched side by side with him thereafter....

It was Marshall who...went to China to execute the criminal folly of the disastrous Marshall mission....

It was the State Department under Marshall...that sabotaged the $125,000,000 military-aid bill to China in 1948.

It was Marshall who fixed the dividing line for Korea along the thirty-eighth parallel, a line historically chosen by Russia to mark its sphere of interest in Korea.

It is Marshall's strategy for Korea which has turned that war into a pointless slaughter, reversing the dictum of Von

Clausewitz and every military theorist since him that the object of a war is not merely to kill but to impose your will on the enemy.

It is Marshall-Acheson strategy for Europe to build the defense of Europe solely around the Atlantic Pact nations, excluding the two great wells of anti-Communist manpower in Western Germany and Spain and spurning the organized armies of Greece and Turkey....

It is Marshall who, advocating timidity, as a policy so as not to annoy the forces of Soviet imperialism in Asia, admittedly put a brake on the preparations to fight, rationalizing his reluctance on the ground that the people are fickle and if war does not come, will hold him to account for excessive zeal....

If Marshall were merely stupid, the laws of probability would dictate that at least some of his decisions would serve this country's interest. If Marshall is innocent of guilty intention, how could he be trusted to guide the defense of this country further? We have declined so precipitously in relation to the Soviet Union in the last 6 years. How much swifter may be our fall into disaster with Marshall at the helm? Where will all this stop? That is not a rhetorical question; ours is not a rhetorical danger. Where next will Marshall carry us?
(Adapted from a McCarthy speech)

What are the charges of McCarthy against Marshall?

Does McCarthy offer any real evidence?

(The Cold War eventually led to an arms race between the United States and the Soviet Union. In 1955 President Eisenhower called for an arms control agreement between the two super powers.)

DWIGHT D. EISENHOWER'S DISARMAMENT PROPOSALS (1955)

I should address myself for a moment principally to the delegates from the Soviet Union, because our two great countries admittedly possess new and terrible weapons in quantities which do give rise in other parts of the world, or reciprocally, to the fear and danger of surprise attack.

I propose, therefore, that we take a practical step, that we begin an arrangement very quickly; as between ourselves—immediately. These steps would include:

To give each other a complete blueprint of our military establishments...

Next, to provide within our countries facilities for aerial photography to the other country....

What specific proposals were made by President Eisenhower?

What has transpired in regards to the arms race since 1955?

Chapter Fifteen
The Struggle for Civil Rights

"Does segregation of children in public schools solely on the basis of race, even though the physical facilities and other "tangible" factors may be equal, deprive the children of the minority group of equal educational opportunities? We believe that it does."—Supreme Court, Brown v. Board of Education (1954)

The 13th, 14th, and 15th amendments were intended to protect the rights of the freedman. However, these amendments were often ignored and failed to protect the civil liberties of the black population in the United States. In terms of political power only a minority of African-Americans were able to utilize their right to vote deep into the 20th century. Moreover, it is a mistake to think of civil rights abuses to have been limited only to the deep South. Ku Klux Klan membership swelled in the 1920's and a good deal of its strength was drawn from the upper Midwest. Prejudice was abundant in the North and the South.

The 1950s marked the beginnings of the modern civil rights movement. The movement, although at times violent, was for the most part a peaceful movement. The emergence of Dr. Martin Luther King was the primary factor in assuring an essentially peaceful movement. The dramatic changes brought about by the civil rights movement of the 50s and 60s mark one of the most turbulent periods in American history.

(Segregation had been given legal sanction in the landmark Supreme Court case of Plessy v. Ferguson in 1896. The "separate but equal" doctrine established by the Plessy case stood for almost 54 years.)

A CASE FOR SEGREGATION

We consider the underlying fallacy of the plaintiff's argument to consist in the assumption that the enforced separation of the two races stamps the colored race with a badge of inferiority. If this be so, it is not by reason of anything found in the act, but solely because the colored race chooses to put that construction upon it.... The argument also assumes that social prejudices may be overcome by legislation, and that equal rights cannot be secured to the Negro except by an enforced commingling of the two races. We cannot accept this proposition.... Legislation is powerless to eradicate racial instincts or to abolish distinctions based upon physical differences, and the attempt to do so can only result in accentuating the difficulties of the present situation. If the civil and political rights of both races be equal one cannot be inferior to the other civilly or politically. If one race be inferior to the other socially, the Constitution of the United States cannot put them upon the same plane.

(From Plessy v. Ferguson, 163 U.S. 537, 1896)

THE CASE AGAINST SEGREGATION

The white race deems itself to be the dominant race in this country. And so it is, in prestige, in achievements, in education, in wealth and in power. So, I doubt not, it will continue to be for all time, if it remains true to its great heritage and holds fast to the principles of constitutional liberty. But in view of the Constitution in the eye of the law, there is in this country no superior, dominant, ruling class of citizens. There is no caste here. Our Constitution is color-blind, and neither knows nor tolerates classes among citizens. In respect of civil rights, all citizens are equal before the law. The humblest is the peer of the most powerful. The law regards man as man, and takes no account of his surroundings or of his color when his civil rights as guaranteed by the Supreme law of the land are involved. It is, therefore, to be regretted that this high tribunal, the final expositor of the fundamental law of the land, has reached the conclusion that it is competent for a State to regulate the enjoyment by citizens of their civil rights solely upon the basis of race.
(From the Dissent of Mr. Justice John Marshall Harlan, Plessy v. Ferguson, 163 U.S. 537, 1896)

On what basis did the court justify segregation?

What importance did the dissenting opinion in Plessy v. Ferguson have?

(In 1954 the Supreme Court overturned the 1896 Plessy ruling in Brown v. Board of Education. The Brown case was a major turning point in the Civil Rights struggle.)

BROWN V. BOARD OF EDUCATION OF TOPEKA, KANSAS

Mr. Chief Justice Warren.... In each of the cases, minors of the Negro race, through their legal representatives, seek the aid of the courts in obtaining admission to the public schools of their community on a nonsegregated basis. In each instance, they had been denied admission to schools attended by white children under laws requiring or permitting segregation according to race. This segregation was alleged to deprive the plaintiffs of the equal protection of the laws under the Fourteenth Amendment...

...The doctrine of "separate but equal" did not make its appearance in this Court until 1896 in the case of Plessy v. Ferguson, involving not education but transportation. American courts have since labored with the doctrine for over a half a century....

In the instant [present] cases...there are findings below that the Negro and white schools involved have been equalized, with respect to buildings, curricula, qualifications and salaries of teachers, and other "tangible" factors. Our decision, therefore, cannot turn on merely a comparison of these tangible factors in the Negro and white schools involved in each of the cases. We must look instead to the effect of segregation itself on public education...

We come then to the question presented: Does segregation of children in public schools solely on the basis of race, even though the physical facilities and other "tangible" factors may be equal, deprive the children of the minority group of equal educational opportunities? We believe that it does.

...To separate them [school children] from others of similar age and qualifications solely because of their race generates a feeling of inferiority as to their status in the community that may affect their hearts and minds in a way unlikely ever to be un-done...

We conclude that in the field of public education the doctrine of "separate but equal" has no place. Separate educational facilities are inherently unequal. Therefore, we hold that the plaintiffs and others similarly situated...are, by reason of the segregation complained of, deprived of the equal protection of the laws guaranteed by the Fourteenth Amendment...

(Brown v. Board of Education of Topeka, 347 U.S. 483 (1954))

(The Civil Rights movement was somewhat split between the forces of violence and non-violence. Under the leadership of Dr. Martin Luther King, the majority of the civil rights advocates chose the path of non-violence.)

A CASE FOR VIOLENCE

There has always existed in the Black colony of Afro-America a fundamental difference over which tactics from the broad spectrum of alternatives Black people should employ in their struggle for national liberation. One side of this difference contends that Black people...must employ no tactic that will anger the oppressor whites. This view holds that Black people constitute a hopeless minority and that salvation for Black people lies in developing brotherly relations....

On the other side of the difference, we find that the point of departure is the principle that the oppressor has no rights that the oppressed is bound to respect. Kill the slave master, destroy him utterly, move against him with implacable fortitude. Break his oppressive power by any means necessary.... The heirs of Malcolm have picked up the gun and, taking first things first, are moving to expose the endorsed leaders for the Black masses to see them for what they are and always have been. The choice offered by the heirs of Malcolm is to repudiate the oppressor...or face a merciless, speedy and most timely execution for treason.

(From Huey P. Newton, In Defense of Self Defense, The Black Panther, July 3, 1967)

A CASE AGAINST VIOLENCE

Probably the most destructive feature of Black Power is its unconscious and often conscious call for retaliatory violence.... The problem with hatred and violence is that they intensify the fears of the white majority, and leave them less ashamed of their prejudices toward Negroes. In the guilt and confusion confronting our society, violence only adds to the chaos. It deepens the brutality of the oppressor and increases the bitterness of the oppressed. Violence is the antithesis of creativity and wholeness. It destroys community and makes brotherhood impossible....

The ultimate weakness of violence is that it is a descending spiral, begetting the very thing it seeks to destroy. Instead of diminishing evil, it multiplies it. Through violence you may murder the liar, but you cannot murder the lie, nor establish the truth. Through violence you may murder the hater, but you do not murder hate. In fact, violence merely increases hate. So it goes. Returning violence for violence multiplies violence, adding deeper darkness to a night already devoid of stars. Darkness cannot drive out darkness; only light can do that. Hate cannot drive out hate; only love can do that.

(From Martin Luther King, Jr., *Where Do We Go From Here: Chaos or Community?*, 1967)

Why did Mr. Newton support a violent movement?

Why did Mr. King argue that violence was the wrong path?

(Perhaps the most stirring Civil Rights speech ever delivered was Dr. King's 1963 "I have a dream" speech.)

I HAVE A DREAM

I say to you today, my friends, that in spite of the difficulties and frustrations of the moment I still have a dream. It is a dream deeply rooted in the American dream.

I have a dream that one day this nation will rise up and live out the true meaning of its creed: "We hold these truths to be self-evident; that all men are created equal."

I have a dream that one day on the red hills of Georgia the sons of former slaves and sons of former slave owners will be able to sit down together at the table of brotherhood....

I have a dream that my four little children will one day live in a nation where they will not be judged by the color of their skin but by the content of their character.

I have a dream today....

Has Dr. King's dream become a reality?

(In some respects the Women's Rights Movement gained new impetus during the Civil Rights movement. The National Organization for Women (NOW) made a plea for true equality in 1966.)

A STATEMENT FROM N.O.W.

We, men and women who hereby constitute ourselves as the National Organization for Women, believe that the time has come for a new movement toward true equality for all women in America, and toward a fully equal partnership of the sexes, as part of the world-wide revolution of human rights now taking place within and beyond our national borders....

WE REJECT the current assumption that a man must carry the sole burden of supporting himself, his wife, and family, and that a woman is automatically entitled to lifelong support by a man upon her marriage, or that marriage, home and family are primarily woman's world and responsibility—hers, to dominate—his to support. We believe that a true partnership between the sexes demands a different concept of marriage, an equitable sharing of the responsibilities of home and children and of the economic burdens of their support....

IN THE INTERESTS OF THE HUMAN DIGNITY OF WOMEN, we will protest, and endeavor to change, the false image of women now prevalent in the mass media, and in the texts, ceremonies, laws, and practices of the major social institutions. Such images perpetuate contempt for women by society and by women for themselves.... WE BELIEVE THAT women will do most to create a new image of women by acting now, and by speaking out in behalf of their own equality, freedom, and human dignity—not in pleas for special privilege, nor in enmity toward men, who are also victims of the current, half-equality between the sexes—but in an active, self-respecting partnership with men.

(From the National Organization for Women, Statement of Purpose, 1966)

What were some of the concerns of N.O.W. in 1966?

How far have women's rights advanced since 1966?

Chapter Sixteen
The Sixties and Beyond

"Let every nation know, whether it wishes us well or ill, that we shall pay any price, bear any burden, meet any hardship, support any friend, oppose any foe to assure the survival and the success of liberty."—John F. Kennedy

Almost sixty years have passed since the end of World War II. Woodrow Wilson's reference to World War I as the "war to end all wars" seems pathetically na¿ve to us looking backwards from the 21st century. Few who listened to John F. Kennedy's inaugural address in 1961 could have imagined the price that we would have to pay over the next forty years to insure world peace. Many have questioned the active role the United States has played in world affairs since the end of World War II. It has been argued that America has pursued its own interests in the name of world stability. Others have pointed out that the interest of the United States is tied to world peace.

America has a propensity to reveal its mistakes to the world. It has been said that this ability to admit our wrongdoing has set us apart from the other nations of the world. As America continues to dominate world affairs in the early 21st century, it seems more important than ever for the United States to evaluate its purpose and methods in carrying out foreign policy. Jefferson spoke of the need for an informed citizenry. Such an informed citizen base is needed now more than ever, given the complexity of the world in the 21st century.

(The words of John F. Kennedy in 1961 inspired thousands of Americans.)

JOHN F. KENNEDY'S INAUGURAL ADDRESS (1961)

We dare not forget today that we are the heirs of that first revolution. Let the word go forth from this time and place to friend and foe alike, that the torch has been passed to a new generation of Americans—born in this century, tempered by war, disciplined by a hard and bitter peace, proud of our ancient heritage—and unwilling to witness or permit the slow undoing of those human rights to which this nation has always been committed, and to which we are committed today at home and around the world.

Let every nation know, whether it wishes us well or ill, that we shall pay any price, bear any burden, meet any hardship, support any friend, oppose any foe to assure the survival and the success of liberty....

Why did so many people find Mr. Kennedy's words so inspiring?

(The Vietnam War was America's most controversial war. The 1964 Gulf of Tonkin Resolution gave the president broad power to conduct the war.)

THE GULF OF TONKIN RESOLUTION (1964)

Whereas naval units of the Communist regime in Vietnam, in violation of the principles of the Charter of the United Nations and of international law, have deliberately and repeatedly attacked United States naval vessels lawfully present in international waters, and have thereby created a serious threat to international peace; and

Whereas these attacks are part of a deliberate and systematic campaign of aggression that the Communist regime in North Vietnam has been waging against its neighbors and the nations joined with them in collective defense of their freedom;.... Now therefore, be it

Resolved by the Senate and House of Representatives of the United States of America in Congress assembled, that the Congress approves and supports the determination of the President, as Commander in Chief, to take all necessary measures to repel any armed attack against the forces of the United States and to prevent further aggression.

How was the president's "war power" increased by the Gulf of Tonkin Resolution?

(The Vietnam War brought forth varying opinions on the morality of war. One of the more controversial aspects of the war was the loss of civilian lives due to American bombing raids.)

A DEFENSE OF VIETNAM

Despite the long years of support and vast expenditure of lives and funds, the United States in the end abandoned South Vietnam. There is no other true way to put it.... After introduction of American combat troops into South Vietnam in 1965, the war still might have been ended within a few years, except for the ill-considered policy of graduated response against North Vietnam. Bomb a little, stop it a while to give the enemy a chance to cry uncle, then bomb a little bit more but never enough to really hurt. That was no way to win. Yet even with the handicap of graduated response, the war still could have been brought to a favorable end following defeat of the enemy's Tet offensive in 1968. The United States had in South Vietnam at that time the finest military force—though not the largest—every assembled. Had President Johnson provided reinforcements, and had he authorized the operations I had planned in Laos and Cambodia and north of the DMZ, along with intensified bombing and the mining of Haiphong Harbor, the North Vietnamese would have broken. But that was not to be. Press and television had created an aura not of victory but of defeat, and timid officials in Washington listened more to the media than to their own representatives on the scene.

(From General C. Westmoreland, A Soldier Reports, 1976)

SPEAKING OUT AGAINST VIETNAM

There may be a limit beyond which many Americans and much of the world will not permit the United States to go. The picture of the world's greatest super-power killing or seriously injuring 1,000 noncombatants a week, while trying to pound a tiny backward nation into submission on an issue whose merits are hotly disputed, is not a pretty one. It could conceivably produce a costly distortion in the American national consciousness and in the world image of the United States—especially if the damage to North Vietnam is complete enough to be 'successful'. (From Secretary of Defense Robert S. McNamara, President Johnson, May 19, 1967)

Discuss the validity of the statement, "Vietnam was America's most unpopular war".

Why was is so unpopular?

(The greatest political scandal of the 20ᵗʰ century was the Watergate Affair, which involved the Nixon presidency. In 1974, the House of Representatives Judiciary Committee voted to have the full House consider the impeachment of Richard Nixon.)

HOUSE JUDICIARY COMMITTEE (1974)

Article I
In his conduct of the office of President of the United States, Richard M. Nixon, in violation of his constitutional oath faithfully to execute the office of President of the United States...and in violation of his constitutional duty to take care that the laws be faithfully executed, has prevented, obstructed, and impeded the administration of justice.... Richard M. Nixon, using the powers of his high office, engaged personally and through his subordinates and agents in a course of conduct or plan designed to delay, impede, and obstruct the investigation of such unlawful entry; to cover up, conceal and protect those responsible; and to conceal the existence and scope of other unlawful covert activities.... In all of this, Richard M. Nixon has acted in a manner contrary to his trust as President and subversive of constitutional government, to the great prejudice of the cause of law and justice and to the manifest injury of the people of the United States.

Wherefore Richard M. Nixon, by such conduct, warrants impeachment and trial, and removal from office.

Article II
Using the powers of the office of President of the United States, Richard M. Nixon...has repeatedly engaged in conduct violating the constitutional rights of citizens, impairing the due and proper administration of justice in the conduct of lawful inquiries, or contravening the laws governing agencies of the executive branch....

Wherefore, Richard M. Nixon, by such conduct, warrants impeachment and trial, and removal from office.

Article III

In his conduct of the office of President of the United States, Richard M. Nixon...has failed without lawful cause or excuse to produce papers and things, as directed by duly authorized subpoenas...and willfully disobeyed such subpoenas...thereby assuming for himself functions and judgments necessary to the exercise of the sole power of impeachment vested by the Constitution in the House of Representatives....

Wherefore, Richard M. Nixon, by such conduct, warrants impeachment and trial, and removal from office.

(From the House of Representatives Committee on the Judiciary, August 4, 1974)

What were the accusations made against President Nixon?

Proof